So Translating Rivers and Cities

So Translating Rivers and Cities
SELECTED POEMS

Zhang Er

Translated by
Bob Holman ¦ Arpine Konyalian Grenier
Timothy Liu ¦ Bill Ransom
Susan M. Schultz ¦ Leonard Schwartz
with the author

ZEPHYR PRESS
BROOKLINE, MA

Cover painting by Emily Cheng
Book design by *typeslowly*
Printed in Michigan by Cushing-Malloy, Inc.

Zephyr Press acknowledges with gratitude the financial support of the Massachusetts Cultural Council.

massculturalcouncil.org

Library of Congress Control Number:

Zhang, Er.
 [Poems. English. Selections]
 So translating rivers and cities : poems / by Zhang Er ; translated from Chinese by Bob Holman ... [et. al].
    p. cm.
 Includes bibliographical references.
 ISBN 978-0-939010-93-6 (alk. paper)
 I. Holman, Bob. II. Title.
 PL2929.5.N417A24 2007
 895.1'152--dc22

                              2007026376

9 8 7 6 5 4 3 2 first edition in 2007

Zephyr Press
50 Kenwood St.
Brookline, MA 02446
www.zephyrpress.org

Table of Contents

姑媱秋
The Autumn
of GuYao

冬日花园
Winter
Garden

妈妈事件
Mother
Event

姑媱秋

The Autumn
of GuYao

女丑

女丑之尸，生而十日炙杀之。在丈夫北。以右手鄣其面。十日居上，女丑居山之上。

—《山海经（海外西经）》

走过溪水的当儿，你没料到
命里注定的厄运——
那金蛇转一转细软的脖颈
朝你嬉笑着游去，踝下文上
一支玫瑰装扮你从此
越发俊俏，眸子黝亮如躺上河床的
鸟卵，孵鹅还是孵鸭事后证明
与花间棘刺浓疏不无关系

都说你生得美，偏偏叫个丑，并且
严密地遮蔽了脸，以至什么都相信
也什么都不相信的我们竟也无端做出
种种揣摩，不知道你穿起为明天剪裁的
鲜亮女制服会不会就能
挺胸昂首，剔除自卑心理，搞活公共关系
并且操一口流畅的太阳系语？

而这只不过刚刚开始，洪水猛兽
簇拥我们走上台阶，并非由于不知趣
或者看不破红尘，正如你居山不下，烧灼烤炙
也未见得锻炼成玄鸟，赤龙或者
铁凤凰。你就是你，却不只是你，双重身份
浸染，你有三泽潭波荡
我有三十样不同风味的套装

NuChou (Ugly Girl)

NuChou was alive, but she was roasted to death by ten suns north of ZhangFu.
Up on the mountain, she used her right hand to shade her face from the ten
suns above.

—The Legend of the Western Lands

Wading in the small stream, you didn't expect
your life's great misfortune—
the golden snake turning its slender neck
swam toward you, grinning, tattooed your ankle with a kiss.
From that moment on, a rose dressed you up
prettier than ever, your pupils sparkling like egg-shaped pebbles.
Whether or not they could hatch ducks or geese on the river bed
later proved related to the multitude or sparseness
of thorns between the flowers.

Everyone said you were beautiful at birth, only to be called Ugly.
Yet you covered your face, so even we skeptics doubted
without particular reason. If you put on a bright colored suit for tomorrow,
will you square your shoulders and keep your chin up, rid yourself
of self-doubt, and speak the language of the stars?

But this is only the beginning; fierce floods and horrible scourges
escort us up the stairs, not because we lack modesty
or are unable to see through the veils of this world
just as your stay up on the mountain, baking and burning,
did not forge you into the magic black bird, red dragon or iron phoenix.

You are you, yet more than that, a double identity,
brim-full, like the waves on the three ponds;

却焦渴依然。太多的表面需要覆盖
太少的根蒂可以系结。轻率步出闺门
易招灾祸，比如撞上十日蒸腾
或者净月林荫道醺醉眼悠扬飞车。
而我们表情过于诚恳也过于青嫩，我们做不出
一步三摇玉佩叮咚透花挑纱再细细镶入
肉红色球穗，欲动种种之后
归宿一袭皂衫，像日久天长
又落满灰尘的婚姻，夕阳下手挽手
更显得有滋有味，好比这童话
自生自灭的前途，其中真伪
除了你我，大家都意见一致。

至于他们的思想动态，你依然不能领悟——
尽管大旱大暴的狂潮已退去多时
心中的太阳也已一一中矢，太阳下面
笔触细腻的百花园一方方整齐奔放
黑领结白领结侍者们肃立恭候
游乐场人如鱼粥，我们疑惑不决登天梯
还是穿莽林，有关中国商市的理论
普照大街小道，一至三十号防晒润肤面霜
充斥我窄窄的浴室，而想象强烈的
追光已暗下去，再暗下去，只有你
其丑难比，郭面千年仍秀色迷人
被我们不断记起，是你吗？
台灯下耳环金蛇暖暖微笑的倩魂？

I have thirty outfits of various kinds
and am still as thirsty as ever. Too many surfaces to cover,
too few roots to clutch. Indiscreetly walking out of the chamber
invites disaster, for example, running into the ten rising suns
or driving carefree with drunken eyes on the tree-lined street in moonlight.
Our expressions are too earnest and naive; we can't do
the three swings of the hip for each step, tinkling jade pendants on cross-stitched
embroidered silk gauze gowns lined with red beads and tassels,
agitating desire. Afterward, return to a plain black dress
as to a long marriage, you and he walking hand in hand
in the setting sun. It tastes better with age, like a fairy tale
that's born and dies in its own course,
and besides, the truth is they have the same opinions.

You still cannot fathom their motives,
even though the maddening cycle of drought and violence long ago subsided;
the cherished suns have been shot down, one after another,
as, under the sun, the Hundred Flower gardens are kept tidy, and bloom.
People swarm to amusement parks like schools of fish,
can't decide whether to brave the roller coaster
or be driven through the haunted forest. The theory
of the vast Chinese market economy illuminates all things.
I keep level 30 sunblock stuffed in my tiny bathroom.
The imagined spotlight has grown faint, is growing more so,
only you are so ugly nothing can be compared to you
nor shade your face for thousands of years;
you will stay as seductive as ever
and we will always remember. Is that you
under the reading lamp with golden snakes in your ear lobes,
a beautiful, smiling soul?

translated by Susan M. Schultz

女娃精卫

又北二百里，曰发鸠之山，其上多柘木。有鸟焉，其状如乌，文首，白喙，赤足，名曰精卫，其鸣自詨。是炎帝之少女曰女娃，女娃游于东海，溺而不返，故为精卫，常衔西山之木石，以堙东海。

——《山海经（北山经）》

柘木拖鞋的传统上溯公元以前
赤红丝带系住赤红足踝，仿佛
一串丹艳的吻，你往返匆匆的异国情调
充满刻意的渊源——
你不是寻常的女娃
根生在骨殖里的泥石场让你
不由得迁徙，自南方走上我家后院的西山
并小声告诉我翻下去的是哪一边

向前，向东海，向着太阳
但这里偏偏缺乏阳光，面皮白嫩，看得出
人人都喝过不少黑咖啡好似
镜子周围的影像和
相片后面的交易，你不得不
有所设防，这里的海湾
胃口很大，不吃石或木料，却热衷于
钢梁与塑料的七巧拼盘——
船艇舰舫舸
以及其中千货百色的玻璃橱窗，游客
和人们手里的快餐饭盒，再往东走，还有
鲨鱼和鱼翅紫参汤
传统悠久，价廉物生猛
一元两份，
让我们分享

NuWa Jing Wei (the baby girl, Jing Wei)

FuJiu Mountain is 200 li farther north. Higher up, the zhe trees are quite plentiful. There is a crow-like bird here with a striped head, white bill, and red feet. It is called Jing Wei. Its call sounds like its name. This is Emperor Yan's daughter, NuWa. NuWa drowned while swimming in the Eastern Sea. That was when she became Jing Wei and carried trees and stones from the western mountains to dam the Eastern Sea. The Zhang River flows east from here.

—The Legend of the Northern Mountains

Zhe wooden slippers predate the Christian era.
Crimson silk ribbons redden the ankle
like the flush of scarlet kisses; you dart back
and forth, possessed of exotic origins.
NuWa, you're no ordinary girl,
for the magnetic field of your rooted bones
makes you nomadic; you walk from the south
up the western mountain of my backyard:
tell me, which side do I climb down?

Go forward, eastward, face the sun.
Here everyone drinks too much coffee, is pale, sun-starved.
Be cautious: there's a secret deal in mirror-images, photos.
And the bay's appetite!
Not for stones or branches, but for steel and plastic puzzles.
Sail boats, ferries, skulls, steamers, ocean liners
(S.S. Thises and Thats), their shop lights, window displays.
Behind glass you see tourists with styrofoam lunch boxes in hand,
while further east, according to legend, there are shark
and shark fin JinShen soups. Fresh, two for a dollar.
Let us share …

码头旁边，另有一番酒幌招摇着
我们紧挨着坐了，他们热切地上下求索
多元视角，却看不出你脚踩
火色木屐，南方的女娃，东海的水酒
中和的结果由本地语言公布，满瓶溢香
你斯文地等了又等
优雅地垂着头，就像每一次失恋
都明白了许多事情，而下一次
只有我知道你的行程：
"一天十二个点钟"
歌喉迷人，虽然不再表现过去的日子
或者入时的歌谣，你勤勤恳恳的啼鸣不止撩动——
他们的想象力
某些行动准则横贯至今天——
仍深似东海和稳居后院的山岭
他们有苦难吐

我家有一个晚会，会上有一些无缘由的
怨恨。祖母突然病逝没有留下遗嘱
却生产过不少遗言和许许多多年代久远的
毛巾，印花图案混沌难解
她不断打电话给我与死去多年的祖父
聊天，一种奇异的体验，好比医生说
你患染子宫颈癌，节食不彻底
多枚爱慕者，还是你父亲遗传因子不佳

"我娃是女娃"，祖母总是自言自语
天上飞，地下跑，水中游
你红丝带赤足拖柘木鞋溺而不返
少年英雄，天才儿童，中学生作文选里

Beside the pier, the winery banner seduces us
to sit, shoulder to shoulder, while other eyes scatter,
multi-angled lenses that fail to mark your fire-red slippers,
southern NuWa, nor their ears the eastern sea wind,
results posted in the local language
like fragrance rushing from a bottle.
You wait, patiently, patiently,
gracefully lowering your head as if
each time your heart broke there were
the consolatory "next time."

Only I know your path:
It's like the song, "12 Hours a Day."
Sweet nostalgia of no longer
fashionable music, about a time
no longer fashionable, whose
ancient principles yet apply,
deep as the eastern sea and this
backyard, bitterness unvomited.

My guests' anger baseless.
Grandma died without a will
despite torrents of last words and piles of ancient
towels, prints smudged, difficult to fathom;
she phoned my grandpa, recently dead,
to chat; the doctor called it "a strange existence."
Your cervical cancer caused by poor water, poor diet,
an excess of love, the deep pool of your genes?
Excess misery and beauty were her company.
"My baby is NuWa," grandma murmured to herself.
Fly, run, swim! Your crimson silk string slippers drown,
young heroine, yet the yearbook leaves out your entry.

却忘记登载有关你的消息，入选的
净是些我们尚未听懂
却已经耿耿于怀的字眼——
"热爱生活"
晚会上披红戴绿，我们哭喜丧——
她八十九岁，你十八九岁

要学那西山顶上一青柘
和枝头其状如乌的鸟，死而有恨正如
古书里的话永远有理，不需要注解
你握着我的手
我面对着那边海天一色
后院山梁人欢马叫，挖山不止——
或以堙东海或以身相许，人们争执不休——
你与我更值得再坐一坐，多斟酌一盅

"精卫"，"精卫"，"精——卫——"

What are collected are as-yet-undefined words,
phrases that already trouble us, like "love life."
At the party, in fancy dress, we cry for a happy funeral.
You see, she was 89; you only 18 or 19.

One should learn from the green Zhe tree on the western mountain.
The crow-like bird in the branches died of hatred.
The ancient book still contains unparaphraseable wisdom.
You hold my two hands in yours.
I face the sky blue sea—over there.
In the backyard and on the hill, crowds bustle and horses neigh.
Hard at work, they dig at the mountain without ceasing,
either to dam the eastern sea or build a new legend.
They quarrel: so you and I have reason to sit longer.
We'll share another mug of wine.

translated by Susan M. Schultz

姑媱秋

又东二百里，曰姑媱之山。帝女死焉，其名曰女尸，化为䔄草，其叶胥成，
其华黄，其实如菟丘，服之媚于人。

—《山海经（中山经）》

　　第二天，叶子们已经决定要变换颜色。 这是一个生或死的折点，
跨出这一步意味着失去逆转的可能。空中迁徙的翅膀闪动，风一阵凉
似一阵，不容再犹豫。变做红与金黄之间的种种层次需要勇气，需要
适当的温差，阳光，水分，需要积极的工作，光合转换，有些成分要
去除，有些要存留，另有一些新鲜分子要从头孕育合成。这是一个主
动的历程，一个忙碌的历程，对于终局的预想以及由此引出的焦躁结
成看不见的阔网，仿若充满张力的气体在叶间营营颤抖，难以分辨何
起何止。

　　不是没有另外的选择，比如不变换颜色，静止等候严冬光临，绝
了希望和快乐，痛心疾首到时间与记忆均无法挽回的地步，然后整体
死去，去死，连枝带叶带根系，一片大山白茫茫，连我们曾否存在都
成为疑问。又如，自生灾祸，长疮害虫不医不治，痛快结束在一丛青
翠之际，留下块高低起伏疙里疙瘩的疮疤，成心恶心的惨烈之象。

The Autumn of GuYao

GuYao Mountain is 200 li farther east. This is where a princess named NuShi died and became the yao grass. Its leaves grow thickly, its flowers are yellow, and the fruits are like those of an herbal medicine. Whoever eats them is seductive.

—The Legend of the Central Mountains

On the second day the leaves made up their minds to change color. A breaking point, since taking this step means there's no turning back. The sky fills with wing beats as the wind grows colder and the time for hesitation dissolves. The shift from red to yellow to in-between shades demands courage and zealous work: it requires the right temperatures, sunlight, moisture, photosynthesis, elimination of some things and addition of others. The new synthesis requires fresh molecules. An active procedure always. Anxiety that's caused by anticipation of the final stage weaves a wide web, like air trembling between the leaves; it's hard to tell what the beginning is, where the end.

It's not that there is no other choice, as if it were possible not to change color, not to give up hope or happiness, to await winter's onslaught quietly, not to be made desperate, inconsolable by time or memory and then to die with the leaves, the branches, the roots, a bleached barrenness. The question is whether we have existed at all. There are, as well, the self-imposed disasters, the sores and infestations, refusals of treatment that leave behind scars, deaths so brutal they can't be faced.

也还可以置一书案，依山搭起木屋，仿先师哲人的私斋。屋旁植栽兰草，石榴无花果，或者什么都不精心，凭自然造化，也会有花果点缀得星星点点。听林石花木，感脉搏心动，体液盈虚。减灭宴乐，声色，名位之后，方可容纳另一空间，纸页上写下的便站成三维世界，任你一直想下去，或轻快前行，或停停走走，岔路口上迂回碾转，不甘心放弃，又明知继续转下去再难有新颖花色。那就向左转吧，要不，就向右转，总有一个契机催促，外部平衡打破，你需要的是耐心与顺水推舟，不断修正航线以至于目的地的本领——既没有可能如诗地长青藤般常青地生存，那么就不要缠绵萦绕，死揪住不放。可是不缠绵萦绕我们只好继续前行，只好改变颜色。

步出屋宇，我走向你们，踏上你们的荫凉，穿行于你们手臂之间，但我知道这只是一种永恒的渐近，也就是说我将永远走不进你们的世界，无论我如何努力刻苦，下血本，功夫深，一步一个脚印，得到的只能是某种失去。我无法把握你，更不能以这种把握成就自己。自己只得或套装制服，或运动衣衫，或猎装牛仔裤，晚礼服长裙袭地之后又织锦睡袍加身，日日角色变换奔忙不已，企图掩饰的不过是一具一穷二白的躯体与灵窍，格调入时，微笑俊美，从早到晚从上到下受人爱戴醒人耳目回头率提高，可是已经有那么多的注意力需要吸引，成千上万，上亿，上兆，上X（？），不必担心，到时候智慧的大脑就有答案等在那里，很自信，很逻辑地继续替我们数下去，一X，百X，千X，谁该不相信人类有无穷的想象力，谁能与我们将一张模版印成千百页书报的本领与耐性匹敌？比如，眼前这片林木，细细看去高低明晦色调姿态千容万方，每一叶片与其他所有叶片都不雷同。秋日里他们浓荫依旧，荫下泥土中深深浅浅藏过我们视线的根茎又孕含着怎样一些源远流长各式各样生生息息的故事？

You can also set up a reading desk, build a wooden house on the slope, mimic the private studies of respected teachers, wise men of the past, plant fragrant thoroughwort beside the house, pomegranates, figs, or let nature choose the fruits and flowers and then listen to the forest, the stones, flowers and grasses, feeling the pulse, the high and low tides of the body's fluids. After abolishing parties and pleasures, fame and status, there will be another place—what is written will stand up in the world dimensional, as you stroll toward the intersection, not giving up but knowing that the circle yields no new design or color. Turn left—no, right!—the surface disturbed as by a stone thrown from nowhere; you need patience and skill to paddle in the current, revising the route as you go, even changing destination—so long as we cannot live like poetry's green vine, we must give up grasping until the bitter end. We can't linger, have to move on, must change our colors.

Leaving the house, I walk into your shade, traveling between your upraised arms, though I can't walk in your world no matter how much I invest in it, how crafty I manage to become. For what I gain in walking toward you is also my loss. I can master neither you nor myself in this place. The self is clothed: I put on a business suit, a sweatsuit, a hunting outfit, jeans, even an evening dress that floats to the ground, or a silk embroidered nightgown. Body and soul's cover-up. Dressed fashionably, the self smiles from morning until night, increasingly loved and respected. Yet attention grows geometrically: there is too much to catch! Who can match our skill, our patience, the hundreds of thousands of pages from a single mold? Just look at these trees, the huge and the small ones, bright and dark; their every gesture shifts, alters, adjusts; every leaf different from its fellows. This autumn day, the shade is still thick with them. Under the soil's shadows, roots deep and shallow hidden from view, what stories of ancient origins lie tethered in this shadowed soil?

即便沿着这山林小径散步，也有的是曲折意外，转念之间不知不觉就可能迈出错误的一步，跨过那条不可逆转的疆界。"没有风险就没有将来"，这个时代的代言人—投资银行家语录，我们将来的风险会是什么？枪杀，车祸，饥饿，疾病，身无分文，一事无成？最终不过是个死，"掉了脑袋碗大的疤"，然而明晓终极不等于解除忧虑，仍旧担心，仍旧烦躁，仍旧接长不短感觉过不了某个坎。"无后为大"的古训也许正是针对这种骨肉凡胎永存焦虑的良药。"有后"将我们的体质与思维方式传下去，使我们轻而易举地超越神与人的界限，睡在床上或提起笔来（轻轻一个跳跃），就迈过所有的坎坷。"有后"才有将来，才有我们泱泱大国的今天，再丰富的人欲物质，不如神仙自在逍遥。"有后"的坦荡实乃温良恭俭让优良品德的根基。我们能忍让如坡上那株黄叶零落而枝干陡挺的橡树，忍气候多变，忍泥土贫瘠，忍水深与火热，忍合理与不合理的密植与砍伐，一忍再忍，忍气吞声直至忍无可忍，连接头脑与躯体的颈子则首当其冲，我们抹脖子，上吊，斩首，将肉体与灵魂分离，"心"安"理"得。各守其位，多亏了细软的脖子，在摆来摆去摆不平的节骨眼儿上给予我们一件轻巧的一次性法宝。

脚下一声脆响，踩裂一只橡子，皮毛油亮的松鼠惊跳窜入树梢，树梢上瓦蓝的一块是外面的天，太阳望去很新鲜，幸而世上有这许多得以分散注意力的事件，事物，食物，当我们找不出感觉又不忍观看北非儿童皮包不住骨头苍蝇落在厚嘴唇上无力驱打的晚间节目，就走去街对面意大利餐馆美美吃一顿滑韧的"天使法"细面条，匀匀浇上番茄蛤肉浓香汁，驶过那位风雨中端坐桥头的残肢老者，不减速不转睛，"闲聊波尔卡"节奏不凡，盘算或许该写几句诗文献给更彻底地远居阳光以外的祖母，心身的潜力不必走极端就分得开灵与肉。

Even strolling disingenuously on this forest path, you might take a wrong step, cross a forbidden border. "There will be no future if you fail to take the risk." Thus spoke the adventure capital investor, infused with our era's truest wisdom. And what shall be our risk, then? Being gunned down or killed in an accident, starving to death, being poor, accomplishing nothing? Death is always the end. "When the head is cut off, only a scar the size of a rice bowl remains." Yet knowing the story's end can't relieve us of our anxieties; we are still agitated, still sense the hurdle that can't be crossed. "The worst offense is having no offspring," says Confucius. This may be the best remedy against our mortal anxiety. "Having offspring" means maintaining our thought lineage; we leap over the barrier between gods and ourselves; either lying in bed or raising one's pen, hurdles are overcome. "Having offspring": doesn't this wisdom lead to country of multitude? Is it not the tradition of having children that perfects our character, fulfilling the five virtues of a Chinese gentleman, that he be genteel, honest, respectful, moderate and forbearing? We endure like that oak on the hill whose yellow leaves are falling, as it negotiates changes of climate, the impoverished soil, the deep water and scorching fire, the planting and the logging. We take it and take it again, swallowing insults until driven beyond our limits. Then we cut the neck that connects mind and body; we strip flesh from soul. Everyone gets what they deserve, after all. Unbalanced, we are given only that one-time connective, that talisman.

A crunch under foot, a squashed acorn, a squirrel with shining fur startling, leaping from branch to branch. At the tree's top, an azure tile, and then the sun. There are so many ways to distract ourselves. We aren't able to find the proper feeling, yet can't bear to watch the TV's poor diet of starving kids in Africa, flies alighting on their lips—but we can cross the street to the Italian restaurant to eat angel hair pasta with red clam sauce. We refuse to turn our heads to see the old man with one leg in his wheelchair by the

比如我就在积习下拐下右面缓降的小道，它将经过一片静静的水沼，丛丛紫萍青藻浮生，黄昏时分还会有通红通红的夕阳燃烧其上，而直行的路将攀绕过一尊原为清洁环境而设置的垃圾桶，瞄准瞄不准的碎瓶子，红红绿绿的塑料袋，还会有大小鼠类出入。想纯归自然并非容易，多少事情走到我们美妙设计以外的去处，这是个连思想的空闲地都难以搜寻的时代。但我可以避开垃圾，依沼边林木，欣赏夕阳跳跃在湖面草叶树梢上的火苗。

叶片飘洒，指令死亡，而它们依旧从容，红彤彤燃成一片，透出一派刻意的确定，像答案或者某种结论，更仿佛大声宣讲没人要听，也没人听得懂的真言。这便是我们终极的蓍草？服之媚于人，也许是某种心甘情愿的牺牲？不知祭于谁？叶子红，树干直，水稳如镜，如纸。

bridge; the radio plays a Vienna waltz, and tonight I may write a poem for my grandmother who more thoroughly abandoned the light. Only intelligence separates the soul from the flesh, doesn't go to extremes.

For now and out of habit I walk to the right, following the slowly descending path, which passes a quiet marsh filled with purple duckweed and green algae floating there with the scarlet sun burning overhead. The straight route would take me by a garbage can, set up to keep the street clean, its bottles and plastic bags a broken aureole near the skittering of mice and rats. Returning to nature is never easy; we arrive at the opposite to our designs. There is no space in which to think clear thoughts. But I can escape the can, lean against a tree beside the marsh, be one with the dancing flames of the sun on blades of grass, the foliage.

The falling leaves are deaths of design, yet they descend gracefully as if to demonstrate their deliberate certainty, an answer, or to broadcast a truth no one cares to hear. Is this our final yao grass? Whoever eats of it is seductive. Perhaps a willing sacrifice? And for whom? The leaves are red, the trees unbending, the water a calm mirror—the page.

羲和

东南海之外，甘水之闲，有羲和之国，有女子名曰羲和，方日浴于甘渊。羲和者，帝俊之妻，生十日。

——《山海经（大荒西经）》

那时候这儿还没有这个园子
你硕硕躺着大声地哼
痛痒交和如原野般铺去，一程复一程
向外的通道窄而扭曲
你停下喘息，向我们招手，又招手
你有的是时间
那时候我们尚在中空浮游
我们居然也仿佛记得
临产巨创意外以内的转折
你要细细缝制儿衣
并为他们和我们垦出这片花园
而你那时耕织的花样儿
我们此时均已无法捕捉

一日又一日，喷涌的火源
将我们的眼底曝光作废
不再存有准确地址
园中几近无花之果和无果之花混居
另有白山与黑水交替插手
早已无力证实九日是否坠地
以及逐日的臆想
现在哪条边缘奔走？
一日又一日，你感情丰富空洞般的脸

XiHe

XiHe's land is on the other side of the Eastern Sea in the Kan River area.
XiHe bathes her suns at the Kan Pool. She is the wife of the Emperor Zun,
and bore him ten suns.

—*The Legend of the Great Beyond to the South*

At that moment, the garden was not here.
Gigantic, you lay, groaning loudly;
pain and irritation stretched out, mile after mile, into the fields.
The passage to the outside is narrow and twisted.
You had to stop, catch your breath, wave to us, wave again.
There was plenty of time.
We were suspended in air,
yet could seem to remember
the unexpected, even within the expected:
you wanted to sew elaborate baby clothes
and plow this garden for them and us—
yet now we can't catch the pattern
of your labor.

Staring at sun after sun, vision destroyed,
we can't keep accurate accounts.
In the garden, infertile fruits and fruitless flowers cohabitate.
The white mountain and black water interrupt each other.
We lost the power to prove if nine suns were dropped to the ground
along with the pipe dream of chasing the sun
as it crosses the border.

在上面浮映，我们匆匆起身
不敢怠慢，看着你的颜色跟着你的步履
停下来就心绪败坏，走起来又苦不堪言
一缕光线，一串机密的波动
你不变的表情是
雾、雨、风和闪电的集成
天热了，天凉了，天亮了
我们言词有限，你并不在意
只耐心地守着我们
不让我们太暖，又不要太冷
这是你的花园
园里面的山岭湖河
已疏导入我们各自独特的梦
是你的，也是我们的

一日又一日，住在凤凰岭的友人打电话
叙述置房买地操办绿卡流程
侵蚀着栽培了一生的
心田和那上面种种细嫩庄稼
水土流失
没有太多绿地可以继续平分
甘水之闲，太阳宫阙却不乏
全场紧逼，冲击防卫，寸土必夺
又深受我们爱戴的绿茵英雄

你同情我们脆弱的营造
不断翻新却永远局促的纸屋
很想满足我们，我们全部小小的心愿
可是向西的窗光线愈加湿润，羞红如
窗棂下即将推开幽暗门户的处女

Sun after sun, the empty fullness of emotions
bob above your head; we get up, not daring to slacken,
watching your mood and following your steps:
guilty if we stop, suffering if we maintain our pace.
unchanged, your expression is
a ray of light, a wave of secret communiqués
amid the fog, rain, wind, lightning.
It is hot or cold or bright
and our vocabulary limited; you don't take
offense, patiently telling us
not to make it too warm or too chilly.
This is your garden,
the hills and pools have already melted in our dreams,
yours and ours.

Sun after sun. A friend from Phoenix calls to say
she's buying land, a house, has the green card.
While the process invades those tender crops
(long cultivation in the heart field)
the green can't be further divided among us.

You pity our fragile creation,
the paper house constantly remodeled yet never comfortable.
You try to satisfy our small desires
but the western light in the window is moist, sun's blush,
as if a virgin leaned there, nearly pushed it open.
All that vividly burns will sink into the dark.
While flowers and bushes fail to conceal time's passage,
you tell us not to worry, overlooking sunlight's final smear.
There will be the next sun; it will illumine
this routine landscape
we have no time to see.

所有生生烧着的都将沉入昏夜
花枝凋谢与时间的远近也许能以
园子外面的草木掩迷，你不想让我们伤心
就这样俯视
慈悲无形，余晖一抹
待明日，又小心沐浴
眼下这幅我们无暇顾及的
日常山水

后　　园

一条土路横上生荒的心
两颗枣树长在我家的后园
果实的汁液意外地流畅
很难说

下种的时候是否在下雨
还是每一只手仿佛都哭过
青椒与小蘑菇如期出土
很难说

收获的时候滋味如何
指甲上总有洗不清的污记
遗失的寓言并没有故事
很难说

捏在手心里的瓦片摔不出一季收成
立在瓦砾上的鸟兽不曾富有
日子石雕般的粗脸是否变老
很难说

Backyard

One dirt road crossing a strayed heart
two jujube trees in the old backyard
the juice of the fruit unexpectedly smooth
it is difficult to say

Whether it was raining when they planted
or as if all the hands had been crying
pakchoi and needle mushroom out of soil on time
it is difficult to say

How they will taste at the harvesting
stains on the nail that never wash away
for the lost fable does not really tell
it is difficult to say

A tile piece hidden in your hand cannot slam into summer
the animals once lavishing by the gravel
whether the old stone face will age
it is difficult to say

女　书

贯穿一致
你袭一身黑衣，偏不甘寂寞
从深沉的河底醒来
很久很久以来

我们一直年轻，也一直惦记着你
沿着雪花飞扬的街巷叫卖热包子
和冻硬的稀粥
很久很久以来

我们只专心地生一个孩子
而且面对没有路障的广场大动肝火
这里应该长树，应该生风
很久很久以来

我们蹲在园子里吸烟，坐在屋子里谈话
议论着你的身世
看着你再一次浸没
你那墨色的纤指

Female Codon

Uniform from head to toe
you in black weary of the barren
rise from the bottomless core of your flow
for a long long time

We always young and always worried about you
running among the snow flakes in the streets hawking
steaming dumplings and frozen porridge
for a long long time

Absorbed in bearing the single child
bawling at the emptied square, no roadblock
here, trees should here, wind should
for a long long time

Squatting in the garden smoking then sat inside
talking about your lineage and ordinates
watching your slender tips once more
soaked in ink

translated by Arpine Konyalian Grenier

女 书

贯穿一致
你袭一身黑衣，偏不甘寂寞
从深沉的河底醒来
很久很久以来

我们一直年轻，也一直惦记着你
沿着雪花飞扬的街巷叫卖热包子
和冻硬的稀粥
很久很久以来

我们只专心地生一个孩子
而且面对没有路障的广场大动肝火
这里应该长树，应该生风
很久很久以来

我们蹲在园子里吸烟，坐在屋子里谈话
议论着你的身世
看着你再一次浸没
你那墨色的纤指

NuShu (Female Script)

all in black
halo to sole
but don't leave
me lone wake
me up oh
from river bed for
a long long time

forever young, us
forever worried we
or remember you
running snowflakes streets
hawking hot Bao/dumplings
Jook/soup get it
while it's frozen for
a long long time

obsessed one child birth
bawling at square of no one
not even a roadblock
there should be trees
should have wind for
a long long time

smoking in the garden
talking in no particular
room yak it up about
ancestors watch you from river bed
dip your finger
black ink
slender

雨　　刷

闲置的冬季
有如他的旗帜
静默中跃跃欲试的手
保持平衡的呼吸

欲望冻僵之前留下片片痕迹
抹是抹不去的
比幻象更纯净的东西
不必精心修饰自己的手套

起伏剧烈的
是把握不定的遗忘
车座上仍旧温暖如去年的春天
和雨季的恐慌提前

以后的事情比意料中简单
不必借助反光镜
他就看清了
站在窗外的自己

Rainwiper

Idly winter
like his flag
silent hand itching to
balance the breathing

Before the chill the traces the yearning left
that cannot be wiped clean
purer than the scenery
no need to flounce the mitten

Up and down and brazen
the randomness of dismissal
backseats still warm from last spring
and the panic for untimely rain

Later unexpectedly simple
without the reflecting mirror
he is able to watch himself
standing, outside

translated by Arpine Konyalian Grenier

绿　袖

没有姓名的艳丽有着
黑丝绒的香馨
以及层层迭迭华彩组汇的
锦绣纹云

紫木檀板惊起一脸羞容
而脱下素白衬裙的程序
依然简明如半扇红漆大门
两只耳坠，一个句点

句子已不再新鲜
那朵金黄色的野雏菊飘走之后
尚未被字迹污染的园子
有覆盆子的猩红和温柔的玫瑰花环

还有吐露着欲望的叶掌
需要花锄的轻抚
如日落时透明的风
拂之生津，浴之不惑

Green Sleeve Beauty

The unnamable
fragrance of black velvet
layer and layer of cloud
embroidered

Sandalwood clappers startled a bashful face
still the stylized motion of removing her white slip
still simple like the leaf of a well lacquered door
two dangling earrings and a period

Sentences ever-new no more
after the dandelion yellow floated away
the garden not yet polluted
tender rose wrath and scarlet raspberries

And the palms unwrap their desire like
leaves of the flower hoe, the feel
like transparent wind at sunset
moistened when caressed, dauntless while soaking

室 内

穿衣镜冷艳之辉构成室内风景
他端详他在镜子里的模样
日复一日
却又日日新鲜

端坐在书架上的
散落成果壳垒砌的混乱
呼吸维艰
他便在花盆里埋下一粒烫熟的果仁

手并不感到疼痛
却无法拾起
行与行之间的热度
剩余的字眼燃点距此不远的

火炉
而他漫不经心堆出的秩序
不可逾越
就像这分开室内室外的门槛

Interior

The glare of the full-length mirror constructs
the chamber he studies his image in
day after day
more sheer by the day

What's on the bookshelf
scattered into the clutter of nut shells
the difficulty to breathe and he
with a scalding nut into the flower pot

His hands do not feel the pain
still unable to pick up
the heat in between lines nearby
the rest of the words inflamed

The stove
while carelessly on a page
the rhythm impasses
a threshold dividing

translated by Arpine Konyalian Grenier

遗　址

出土的不仅是祖宗的假面
还有我们自己不可以示人的脸
在没有了城的墙上悬置
我们有我们的理由

浪漫的手势
以及时时刻刻被注视的感觉
追踪着掘墓人的镢头
我们有我们的理由

为了挖开那条水脉
泥土的润泽已暴晒成沙
渴望生存以致城堡倾斜
我们有我们的理由

重新命名这条遗失了名字的街巷
再细细辫好散乱已久的发髻
假面下的笑容日益纯正
我们有我们的理由

Ruins

The family masks were excavated
but also our faces that cannot be shown
hanging over a city wall without a city
we have our reasons

Exaggerated movements
and the sense of being watched minute by minute
following the grave digger's peg
we have our reasons

To dig for the wellhead
moist soil bleached to dry sand
desire has tilted the castle
we have reasons

Rename these streets that have lost their names
carefully braid long-tangled hair
the smile under the masks more and more genuine
we have our reasons

中国蜂蜜

—给Liz Story

绵延不绝的故事，发生过的
和将要发生的
过去，小心挪动触角，手指
没有折点，东方妇人的皮肤
水蛇出没，曲线游移，洞穴
游戏，音符，文字，游戏，无声的
歌流向脚趾，靛蓝的尖舌，寒彻骨髓
冰河隐伏，热唇裸露
大红床单紧裹不确定的情绪，伸缩如旗
梦游者漠然踱步，腰部柔软
夸张地呻吟

绵延不绝的铃鼓
从一个点到另一个点，思维
不连续的轨迹，没有缓冲
星象，掌纹，激光透视，心理治疗，认知
面目全非，你无言以对
歌一行行漂去
世纪前的缠绕仍缠绕不清
藤蔓，发丝，流水，蔓藤
山的高度陡然迷蒙
破碎的极顶伸张铜锈斑驳的
手指警醒地亲吻花露，异域
风绵延不绝

中国蜂蜜

Chinese Honey

Endless stories
        happened   will happen
the past carefully shifting its antennae
a caressing hand unaware of limitation
        a beautiful Asiatic skin.
Female, the snake merges and emerges
        in a wandering arc; from her cave
        come notes, plays on words.
Soundless song
lapping at the toes, a pointed
indigo tongue, abrupt chill.
Icy river—hidden—exposed warm lips:
        scarlet bed sheets
uncertainty, sweeping back
        and forth like a flag.
The dream walker strolls indifferently
        flexible of waist, exaggerated of moan.

Endless drum beats
   from beat to beat
thought on discontinuous track
     without cognition:
Line by line the song drifts,
twiners of the last century still twining,
        wisteria, long hair, running springs.

The heights of a mountain lost in the haze
        the broken peak vigilantly extends its rusty fingers
kissing the flower dew, the exotic land
Endless wind.

Chinese honey.

translated by Leonard Schwartz

第五种取向

也许折一只纸鸟是最后一招了
翻上翻下总不如意
"东方属木"，她宣布
太阳神庄严的嫩脸
涂上一层绿色就变成了你
剪下的那片枯黄的叶子
飞翔云际
放逐多年自牧成羊
牧童的歌流传至今
披上狼皮
不过为了发出狼腔
颤颤巍巍依然带着羊的口音
不属于狼
另外一种
眼睛闪着格言的诡秘
不必急于辩论太阳的性别
变性手术是这个世纪伟大的发明

昨天被你踢疼的石子
今天长成一张哈哈大笑的嘴
还要再玩一遍吗？
变完魔术，说完相声，洗脸，浣手
出兵，收兵，大打出手，和平演变之后
还要再玩一遍吗？
愤怒都多余
索取说明书

The Fifth Direction

Perhaps the only salvation is folding a paper bird—
even if to fret with paper never brings much content.
The east is wood, she declares.
Face of a Sun God, solemn yet tender—
painted green, it becomes you.

Leaves aloft among the clouds
one shepherds oneself into being the sheep
that puts on the wolf skin,
impersonates the voice of the wolf
still stutter with the voice of the sheep—

No longer the wolf
no longer the sheep
but a third pair of sparkling eyes
and questionable aphorisms.
No use disputing the gender of the sun.
Such confusions did not exist in those days of "glory."

The pebble you kicked and hurt yesterday
turns into a tittering mouth today—
do you want to go out some more and play?

Wave the magic wand, tell riddles
then wash your face and hands—
invasion, retreat, armed assault, painful evolution.
Want to go out some more and play?
Anger does not count.
Ask for instructions

智力游戏
人死了，气不能短
细则一定要读懂
"东方属木"，她重复着，不屈不挠
眼泪也白流
不是所有的枯萎都能再次抽芽
变性手术亦无力回天
埋了，朽了，忘了，记了
就结束了吗？
结块的油脂浮动在盛宴后的盘碟上
消瘦的肋骨成排地乞讨
一些伟大的字眼飘荡得惊心动魄
宛如鸟语
纸笼里的生活也是一种生活
更适于做梦
印在镍币上的依然是汉字
重新掷一次吧
追寻千载难逢的机率
"太阳正照在你头上"，她高叫
不错
添一根重如泰山的羽毛
再作一次有关翱翔的更为华丽的演说

东方属木，南方属火，西方属金，北方水

in the game of wit,
better off dead than without it.

The East is wood, she declares.
Nor do tears count
since what withers cannot always sprout again
and even plastic surgery cannot bring back new life.
A culture buries, rotting, forgotten, "resurrected"—
these are the four directions?
Greasy clots float on the banquet of history's after-dishes
while the poor continue to beg
eloquent with sorrow and pity,
a twittering in their throats like that of birds.

Life inside a paper cage is a kind of life
best suited for the dream
but a sign printed on a venal coin
                    is still a sign
Let us flip it once again
searching for one generation out of a thousand
The sun is shining on your head, she cries out
OK, fine
add a feather heavier than a cliff
make another speech about the art of flying.

The East is wood, the south is fire,
the west is metal; north means the water.

translated by Leonard Schwartz

古事问

光的背后
是坚硬如石的卵
是瞳如深水的眼

光的背后
有风
有白日的异想，没有夜的确定

季候性的水族密集成阵
沉稳地循游
步步逼近脉冲边缘

混沌不定，无动无静
庞然
中心，一只尚未受精的巨卵

剥去坚壳，向内部窥视
穿过浆液，插入弹动的原核
自射之箭指向记忆积层

向外部飞去
向洪玄张开
下一世纪的星蜂拥倒转，雾瀑迷离

企图固化时间的眼执迷于
那行诗句的温柔，那只草莓的红粉，那次云雨的欢愉
一尊窄小的墓碑

Story

Behind the light
there is an egg as hard as stone,
an eye, its pupil the depth of water.

Behind the light
there is the wind,
the reverie of day, not the certainties of night.

Seasonal sea-life in compact formation
calmly cruises by,
steadily approaches the periphery of the pulse.

Void, static yet in flux,
the colossal
center, a giant ovum unfertilized.

Peel off the hard shell, peep into the interior;
penetrate protoplasm, thrusting into the throbbing nucleus:
the arrow of vision reversed in the direction of memory.

To be flung towards an exterior,
to open up to an impenetrable torrent
swarm and swirl of the next centuries' stars,
        misty waterfall.

Attempting to freeze time, eyes transfixed
by the sensuality in one line of a poem,
pinkness of strawberry, comfort after love-making:
        narrow tomb.

青草蔽天
最早的泥土结不出粉红的诗句
只见萤火虫发光的尾部，和不安宁的地衣

在脚下滑移
两块玉石撞击
沉淀在骨骼里的经文，耳廓燥热

反复抚摸光滑如卵的石
仓惶若瞽者震颤的手指
黑暗吞食黑暗

如果天是地，阴是阳，东是西，水是火
则我亦非我，知亦非知
这一边亦那一边吗？

玄武岩上透明的枯叶沉睡如思
随意解析太极之圆
五彩四溅

有梦
将玄学的嫩枝任意组合着
河龟背上十三条甲纹，凶吉非常卜

河神失落
原雨蒸腾
唯一的独木舟早已演为缤纷的水族

大泽浮世，瞳孔迅速下潜
余下的问讯窿张天穹，鱼坠如雨

Green grass blots out the sky
older soils know nothing of this pinkish poetic
only the fluorescent sparks
        of the fireflies, the ancient lichen.

Slidings under the feet.
Two pieces of jade tinkle
a chant is tripped from the bone,
        the ear unrides.

Caress the stone tablet as smooth as an ovum:
letterless hands shaking like those of the blind.
Darkness swallows darkness.

If heaven is earth, yin is yang, east is west, and water, fire,
the self become the nonself, the known, unknown,
and this, that, for sure?

Leaves asleep in mineral thought
casually spun on the wheel of events,
the splashes of color.

A dream
composes at random the tender branches of Thought
into the thirteen cracks on a turtle shell,
        pattern of divination.

God of rivers that sinks into oblivion,
original rain vapor:
an ark becomes the sea.

微光从背后环抱

猛回身
空无一物，闷雷
起自单立之蛋，巍挺若坚岩，有风

Land emerges, the pupils submerging.
A sky created by questioning, fish falling like rain.
A dim light embracing it all from behind.

Turning suddenly
there is this nothingness, muffled thunder
arising from the egg towering like a cliff

And there is the wind.

translated by Leonard Schwartz

冬日花园

Winter Garden

Eclair 咖啡馆

合上书页　我看见　诗
冉冉升起　你　手指纤细
水晶的笑靥
——"今天天气不错"
"不错，不错
一刻胜过一刻。"

咸肉炒蛋　咖啡壶　蒸汽
影爬上墙　不碰　不扰动
袅袅　化简若线　点
光簇移幻　谱调已难
识辨

讲话　聆听
你在中间　不依　不饶
蛋糕——面包与饼干
墙镜——风格与时尚
诗　写与不写
红鼻头男人　红头发女人
你的削肩
"今天天气不错。"
虽然我一直不愿问起
外面雪是否停落
太阳是否暖和
此刻　你我相逢
白色的节日　人群
重编父亲与母亲的故事
就在这里！你和我
也许不

Eclair Café

closing the pages   I saw   the poem
slowly lifted   you   slim-fingered
your crystal smile
—"the weather's not bad today"
"not bad at all
and getting better by the minute"

bacon and eggs   a coffee pot   steam
shadows on the walls   unacknowledged   untouched
bending upwards   simple lines   dots
light shifting tones   difficult now
to comprehend

speaking   listening
you're in the middle   don't move
cake—bread or biscuit
mirror—style or fashion
poetry   written or not
red-nosed man   red-haired woman
your lovely shoulder

"the weather's not bad today"
but I don't want to ask
if the snow outside has stopped
if the sun is still warm
the moment you and I meet
a white holiday   crowds
rewriting a father and mother's story
right here!   but you and I
maybe not

耐心奉上　暗地里　你迟疑的选择
一道又一道
水晶的笑靥　水晶晶
"我不过是你的女侍
不宜审评　增删　发表议论
更不回答画在你本子上的花能否
在下一世纪柔软绽放"

such patient service   as you hesitate   selecting
one course after another
your crystal smile   crystallizing
"I am only a waitress
not a critic   and shouldn't edit   comment
nor answer whether the flower sketched in your notebook
will softly bloom a century from now"

Michi 美发屋

八百间屋宇　千滴花露
调和出美丽与自然的空间
——与宇宙相关
像叶心蜜糖香茅香波
美发师衣襟上脂渍
细述容颜亮丽的秘诀
水性胶　护发素　乳冻　喷丝
今春的发型越直越俏
一丝一扣剪　一条一缕染
你天然发色是碳是墨还是 ESPRESSO？

吹忪　油润　再点开几番层次
出亮　出型　出色
吃透自然　反复雕砌　才美
消减毛重　梳理飞檐
画报上哪幅聪明的模样
你必须挑拣？
烫发液氨碱刺激　热风　表皮牺牲……

所有被我们轻慢翻过的面孔
小心剔除的情爱　字眼　约会　外出与家居
衬托这殷实的下午　偏信　确凿
和镜子里光辉如新的偶像——
假如我们作过另外的选择
拢未被选中的发式
活不是现行的生活
这屋宇下事物将怎样存在
折射怎样的光影？

Michi Beauty Parlor

eight-hundred roofs   and dew from ten-thousand flowers
mediate the space of beauty and nature
taking part of the universe

a honeysuckle lemon-grass shampoo
a cream-colored stain on the hairdresser's sleeve
hold the secrets to looking good
a styling gel oil-free   conditioners   mousse   and spray
the straighter this spring the better
one strand cut after another   one strand dyed then another
is your natural color carbon, ink or espresso?

blow drying   stretching   working through the layers
shine   shape   shade
diving deep into nature   endless sculpting   then the beauty
reduce the volume   trim the edges
what's the latest style
you must pick?
an alkaline ammonia perm   hot air   martyred skin

all the glossy pages we turned over
got erased   relationships   words   going out or staying
gathered into an emptiness   a negative
offset by this solid afternoon   prejudicial   absolute
to behold the brand-new image—
if only we had made other choices
fashion a style we left alone
to live a life not present
beneath this roof   what things might then exist
to refract the light and shadow?

女 人

—川端康成《千羽鹤》读后

1.

一方图案难以走入刻意营造的现实。
瓶插牡丹与淡色麝香石竹指望被宽恕，
寻求的并不是某种完美，恒久或不恒久。

词带着霉味返潮，上下把玩旋转膝头的故事。
不能够承受，室外长疯的花园
已无法理解剪裁的残酷。手绢误入天堂。

从来也不仅是种爱好：茶巾，木炭，云纹笔洗
纸没有阻力，任羽翅在笔记本上写意，
弱者的引诱让我过早微笑。

2.

如果只是两性较力的把戏，
为什么非要格守单一模式？歧意千行，
只凭雄性驱动就能保持艺术对称？

双轨沿同一重心连续。不堪依法沉重，
真实铺出表面簇新的宽街。一笔删除记忆，
便可领会春风擦摩加油站，收款卡，信号灯。

孕兔被无辜碾压，使推理过程显得可疑，
虽然理论的遗传并不缺乏其它反证。
让车轮追赶车轮吧，你说什么？我听不清。

A Thousand Cranes

—reading Yasunari Kawabata

1.

Pattern can't fit into a carefully constructed prism.
Cut peonies and pale carnations want to be forgiven,
Don't yearn for perfection, eternal or no.

Words come back mildewed, fingering a tea cup balanced on the knee.
The garden is overgrown, it no longer understands
The cruelty of pruning. Mistaken handkerchief in heaven.

Nothing is mere hobby: tea napkins, charcoals, ink-dishes nursing clouds.
The page offers no resistance, the poet's feather pen writes freely,
I smile too early at the seduction of the weak.

2.

If it's only a power game between the sexes,
Why this single model? Interpret a thousand lines.
Can the male drive alone give art balance?

Train tracks move along the same center of gravity. Unable to bear the weight,
Truth melts: it's the street's still wet surface. In one stroke, delete the memory,
Then feel the spring breeze caress gas stations, toll booths, signal lights.

The flattened body of a pregnant rabbit fails to mean. Deductive procedures dubious,
There's no shortage of counter-evidence from inherited theory.
What did you say? Let the wheel chase the wheel? I can't hear you.

3.

花园的真贞令人疑惑。太多浓稠的比喻：
牵牛花，杜鹃花，郁金香，风信子，野草莓……
有谁写下这些名字，还能遵循旅行指南？

花落在纸上，散入拒绝吸收的空间。
位置充满暧昧，花非花，墨非墨，
随着假设的改变，不断更换血肉和字迹。

不可能天真无邪。一朵朵像荷莲竞放的
乌鸦也是花园里的鸟，却不按你的欲望依人。
纸上园景公开渲染，竖成无耻的花体广告。

4.

必须把图案看成图案，才能想象雪鹤的群舞。
或许我们应该更挑剔一些，
求偶的固定格局在词的深处抖动。

政治上的一贯正确和无阻力挺入同属谎言。
墨汁自水笔滴下，不涉及没有岸的漂泊。
天真的白纸黑字永远无法逼真自己。

不一定非下海才能看见水。清茶淡墨也是水。
看水时，眼睛会全面崩溃。
故事只有一个：茶碗玉碎完成茶壶罪孽的永生。

translated by Susan M. Schultz

3.

Question the flowers' chastity. There are too many metaphors
In the morning glory, the scarlet star, wax flower, wild strawberry...
Who could write these names down and still follow the guide?

Flowers fall to the page, scatter, refusing space.
Their position is ambiguous, for a flower is no flower, ink no ink;
Premises change with shifting petals and handwriting.

It's impossible to be naïve. Lotuses compete like crows,
Birds in the garden who turn back your desire.
The painted garden is an exaggerated advertisement, and shameless.

4.

One must regard pattern as pattern to imagine the dance of snowy cranes.
Perhaps we should be pickier,
Mating rituals shake through the depth of our words?

Political correctness and entering without resistance are both lies.
The ink that drips down the fountain pen isn't related to shoreless drifting.
Innocence can never face itself, even written in white and black.

To watch water, you don't have to go to the sea. Tea and ink are also water.
Eyes crumble, watching water.
There's only one story: to complete the eternity of the kettle
the tea bowl must be broken.

一 小 块 黄 油

钢琴师的激情倾注餐室
空无一人　天亮得耀眼
等待　如高脚杯　碎冰　白瓷碟
海蓝桌布和瓷碟上一小块黄油
许多事情正在发生　（有象或无象）
从缓慢而坚硬里深化出我们的感觉
我只知道这里能找到安宁
家　女人哭泣　在不远的地方
在不远的地方　今天是情人节
依旧可以独隔玻璃看车与人流

时光　人丛中我找不到你的头
105街和百老汇　超越臆想的座位
维多利亚式桌腿不同地复迷：
像框里空无一人的下午
（电扇在清凉的上空　空旷旋转）
过去的结局和今后的面包片
抹不抹随意　自由
此刻竟如此清晰：柔软　淡黄
不具备另外的表里

音乐的流程缓书这有形的世界
仿佛真地听见了
那位与我面目相同的旅行者
推小车　背具体的行囊（后代婴儿）
在前面的十字路口等候信号：
光的角度？
某种与意识无缘的效果？

Un Petit Beurre

a pianist who fills this café full of feeling
emptiness   a dazzling sky outside
wait   a Champagne glass   a bed
of crushed ice in a dish with a pat of butter
at rest on a sea-blue table cloth   so many things
are happening now   slow and solid
melting down   feelings deeper
wherever peace can still be found
where home is a woman crying not far from here
not far at all   Valentine's Day
looking out alone at a stream of cars and faces

still can't make your head out from the crowd
105th and Broadway   seated
above it all where Victorian-styled table legs
repeat   an afternoon in a photo frame
a ceiling fan rotating the empty air
where future slices of bread come buttered
or not   this moment so free   so soft
pale yellow all I have to contend with
while a stream of music writes this world of forms
as if one could really hear that traveler
whose face resembles mine
pushing a stroller on ahead   something real
waiting at the intersection for the signal
to change   light's angle not related
to thinking?   or a flower stand
whose high prices the roses indulge
even on Valentine's?   as water without structure

花摊上高价红玫瑰自信矫情——
今天情人节？
像水一样没有结构　还是像一小块黄油
别无选择站立　圈定自己的阵脚
再可塑地（从里面）探头探脑？

然后　以完成的动作最后一击
你进入钢琴　（啊！安静）
舌尖上剩下一小块黄油
被我们扭曲　难以辩认的原型
凉　但已经很温柔

or a pat of butter standing without choice
defines its own ground   so supple
from within a finished gesture   looking about
afterwards   till a final pounding

as you enter the piano once again   in peace
a taste of butter on the tip of your tongue
in a form you'd hardly recognize
cool   but already very tender

translated by Timothy Liu

蓝

—献给Krzysztof Kieslowski

有一种与祈祷相仿的情结
点燃纯白的蜡烛，太晚了
我们曾计划将来某个地方　大雪覆盖
深红布景下坐　坐下来休息
吸烟　喝咖啡或茶　听雪
轻松唯美又讨人爱的　嗓音
你被墨水弄脏手指　才发现河对岸
素纸折迭的房屋　实实在在浮出

这生死之谜召唤　不容你拒绝
水汽蒸蒸　一座空桥探出我窗里
望不见的红灯塔：
苍白帆　苍白船
苍白如雪舵手的脸：艰难　刚毅　抒情
歌声像伤疤　自不明高处
像水银灯　忽暗忽明
起桨　落桨　起桨　落桨
如果没有风景，雪还会落下来吗？

听我说，你听我说
虚拟走过场的不止是你
我听到消息　已经太晚
戏装　戏词　戏与戏之间　你划去……
对这个上帝失望
并不是我企图捕捉的词句
"你拾到了就是你的"

Blue

—for Krzysztof Kieslowski

a feeling akin to prayer
ignites the candle   too late
to meet at a certain time and place covered with snow
on a crimson set   take a seat
smoke   drink coffee or tea   listen to the snow's
soft voice   your finger stained
with ink from the other side of the river
where paper houses are folded
into a mystery of life and death you can't refuse

as steam rises from the window   an empty bridge stretching
to a lighthouse that must be there
pale sail   pale boat
the face of the helmsman pale like snow
a song like a wound broadcast from an unknown place
with limelights on   then off
row row   row row
if there is no such place will snow still fall?

listen   won't you listen
it wasn't just you passing through fictitiously
when I heard the news   too late
for lines rehearsed backstage where you rowed away
"disappointed with a god"
and words better left unsaid
"you found it   it's yours"
like a mystery play with an ending preordained?
blue foil   postage stamp   glass frame

那么，一出神秘剧结果预定？
水果糖纸　邮票　眼镜框　雨湿的纱巾
一河摇动　摇动的显影
"你在哭？"
"不，是水。"
不，是葱花在案板上吹口哨。

窗外　更远的地方　更远
长笛和以前对影像的依赖
已强迫我们此岸的今晚　重新进入？
大雪托起烛的晚宴
那最后的辉煌总不该属于眼泪！我太晚
不得不扰动纸中雪景
太晚　你却坚持
背真金十字架　渡河
睁大眼睛我望着你——
天压在上面
不得不呈现　本色

a river rocking with images that soaked into a handkerchief
"are you crying?"   "it's only water"
cut scallions whistling on the countertop

beneath a window that reaches out into the far   farther
but the sounds a flute tonight   and images
bring us back to shore?   again
where the snow serves up a candlelit dinner
unsullied by tears?   too late
to stir that snowy scene on the page
too late   you still insist
on carrying your cross of true gold across the river
with eyes open wide as I watch you
under a sky that presses down from above
showing us all   its true color

translated by Timothy Liu

冬日花园

"从这里进入的
将被神永世诅咒。"
但你可以有多种选择
正步向前或旋身

在真空里哇哇大哭
不会有声音栖落这凋零的园子
园中景物依稀可辨如前世梦境
你不过刚刚出生
周围的冷静就使你怀念起
出生以前的躁动
那时候你四壁禁箍
那时候你拥有一种叫做家的闷热

不愿做奴隶的花匠，揭竿而起
早已在冬天到来之前溃散
从此无人再为你梳妆
从此你也不再记得自己的模样

结冰的湖面只供悼吊遗容
仿佛是一道悟不出的咒语
墨迹斑驳的石碑
牢牢卡住你的喉咙

Winter Garden

I

Whoever enters time
earns God's permanent curse.
But also a whirlwind of choice:
to march forward or swiftly aboutface

Wailing loudly in the vacuum of the garden.
No sound to perch on in this withered place,
the scenery dimly recognizable
as in the dream of a previous life
       or the instant before birth.

The surrounding calm makes you miss
your restless pre-natal movements:
A period in which four walls encircled you
One you were with the stifling warmth of home

But then the gardener, no longer willing to be enslaved,
       lifted his shovel in rebellion
departed well before winter arrived
from then on, no one to dress you
       no memory of your own appearance.

Icy lake sends back an image of mourners.
Incantations go uncomprehended.
A stone tablet engraved with marks whose message
takes hold of your throat, then strangles

不可诉
也不可不诉
只是没有声音
冻土之中，你全力挣扎

何处下种以及何处生根
是你的选择，也是你的职责
而越冬花茎的孕期
并不会因此缩短

一百年后
逃亡的花匠变作游客
而你，永远走不出这冬日花园
世代为奴

II

你已经习惯于一览无余的灰色
和挂在枯枝上去年秋天干瘪的果实
少年少女的嬉笑已铸入青铜
了却开花结果的热闹
无人打扰的园子
用令人羡慕的专注
环抱自己无遮掩的赤裸

家的感觉离你很远，很远
你也不再记起开花的词句
空白中的空旷
平淡如水

Cannot say,
cannot do without saying
soundless in the frozen soil,
you struggle

Where to plant the seed, where to strike root
a choice, a duty
to which the gestating flower
never adapts.

A hundred years later
exiled gardener now a tourist
but you who never stepped out of the winter garden
remain enslaved for generations.

II

Already accustomed to the gloom,
to withered fruit still hanging from the tree.
Children's laughter now cast in bronze.
The turbulent joy of flowering and fruiting is finished.
The undisturbed garden, devoted,
Embraces its own bare flanks.

A sense of home is worlds away.
You no longer remember the names of flowers.
A Nothingness as plain as water—
a drop more would irritate the eye.

多一点都显得刺眼
你满载意念坐了又坐
沉着如园中那无牵无挂的长椅

果实坠地引出的所有经历
仅仅成为某种体验
每一粒灰尘
或许都可以成为再生的核心
不再令人畏惧的毁灭
不再被奉为神灵
习惯死寂的你
在根茎泛青的时刻痛苦万状

拥挤的绿
将不可避免地再次侵入你稀疏的毛发
陌生感在最熟悉的窝里
巨大得吓人
逃是逃不掉的
连头上的天空也被失去控制的枝丫
划成与以往不同的图案

那时候
那孩子拔出水枪随意一摆
你就皮毛蜕落
体内不断发出清脆的爆响
那时候，你就闭上眼睛
你就会看见这安详的冬日花园

You remain rooted to your seat, full of conceptions,
as disinterested as the bench itself.

All events induced by falling fruits
are par for the course
any dirt particle
a potential nuclei of rebirth
a destruction no longer to be feared
abolishes the spirit of worship
you are too used to death and stillness
to suffer pain
when roots and branches turn green.

And the crowd of foliage
could not help but invade your thinning tops
the strangeness in the most familiar nest
startles you with its largesse
no way to escape
a sky divided into
patterns other than the past
branches out of control.

All at once
a boy pulls out a water gun and casually waves it
you slough off your hair and skin
the sound of explosions in the body

All at once you close your eyes
you can see this winter garden serene again.

translated by Leonard Schwartz

渔 人 与 作 家

一

这条路我总走错：出地铁往西
就误入东方的中国城，黑咖啡
酸辣汤，餐桌花瓶里也埋着镇鱼的冰。
混淆的汤水，鲜花与鱼腥。

只有我一个茶客，明亮的地板，手绘彩漆
方桌。书没人翻动，每人都可以是一部。
今天钓上来的鱼，昨天早已制过标本
装了镜框，钉上墙。

河依然从窗外流过，桅杆竖立在巨型家俱店
后面，与我相隔源源不断的街。龙骨悬空
空为某种头上的情致。没见过渔人，或者作家
也许他们病了，也许他们已经出城。

诗流于这混杂的日常，清洁如旧的
布置。走进来的都是过路人，不着急地
吐纳——安然已经美丽，即便没有漆花
香花。诗是城。

只是这条路总错，不断犹疑的坐标
像沙漠季河，渔人每十年走出来一次
用鱼干换佐料，粮米和书，这碟急需的青菜
证明，他们回来了，拎一小串诗。

Anglers and Writers, Hudson Street

1.

Always get the way wrong: exiting the subway to the west
end up in Chinatown to the east: to black coffee,
hot and sour soup, iced fish, ice-filled flower vase
on the table. Blurry liquid, fresh flowers, fish.

I'm the only one for tea. Lacquer table, shiny
wood floor. No one ever riffles the pages here, everyone can be
a book. Today's catch—yesterday's cast—hangs
framed, on the wall.

The Hudson flows beyond the window, masts erect
behind the furniture depot, past the street's incessant traffic. A boat's hull
suspended in air, empty, as a mood. I've never seen an angler or a writer here;
perhaps they're sick, or they left the city.

Poetry blurs unto the blurred routine, old, yet clean.
Passersby walk in, breathe easily; at ease is already
beautiful, even without the painted flowers,
fragrant flowers. Poetry is a city.

But this is the wrong way, maps like moving dunes
a desert river which emerges every ten years, with anglers
exchange dried fish for spices, grains and books; this dish of urgent greens
proves they've returned with their string of small poems.

二

还是先确定自我的身份，生产者－消费者
兼顾？出海时你看见什么？看不见鱼
上钩的是鱼死的过程。非常难过，却出神
张着嘴，因为你不可能控制两极化冰。

船板咯吱咯吱在脚下挣扎，时刻准备
离你而去。除了站着，小心垂下
这偶然一线，你只能高举双手，希望
更像祈祷，愿你为我殷勤的姿态殉情。

这难道不如一次婚约——
茫茫复盲盲，丢个眼波给过路的鱼
你和他一口把月亮咬住，咬紧不放
海浪翻身，连太阳一起抓落。

退潮时，你们对坐桌旁，不经意地剖开
彼此，把每根神经从头嚼到尾，还有心肝
和不再看见的眼珠。听得见肠胃
叽咕，直到彼此全部吃掉，首尾嵌合。

每次下网，都找不到水，因为月历的关系。
每一条鱼，布满刺，非出血才香。鱼汤
溶入所有想象，月光，血光，尝一口
尝一口，你就数得出月亮下所有的浪。

2.

First fix your identity, whether producer, consumer
or both? What do you see out on the sea? You don't see fish.
Who dies on the hook, mouth hinged wide in a desperate
process: you can't control the arctic melting.

Boat's wooden deck squeaks, struggles, threatens to leave you
behind. You stand, carefully let fall
this accidental thread, pressing palms together—more in prayer
than in hope—please do sacrifice yourself for my ardent pose.

It's not unlike a marriage contract,
this sense of being out to sea, blind, throwing
glances to passing fish; you and he both bite down on the moon
refuse to let go, as waves turn to drag down the sun.

At low tide you sit across the table, heartlessly
dissecting each other, chewing every nerve from end to end
heart, liver, and eyes that no longer see. The gut's rumble
heard, until all is eaten, inlaid from head to tail.

Not every net finds water in this lunar calendar.
Every fish has bones, delicious when it bleeds. Fish soup dissolves
the imagination, its moonlight, bloodlight, the one taste that enables
you to count each and every wave beneath the moon.

三

在我们的推断里，生活曾经淳朴——
渔人与作家，这个海滨城市真正需要的
职业。可眼下打鱼不如卖鱼，不如端上桌面的
小小卖弄。一眼便认出这个季节流行。

他曾经让人们在水边满足，从而跟他进入
天堂。现在，地上的我一边没水一边没顶——
闪光发亮、无穷尽计算、声嘶力竭之后，把心
抛向何方？真地钓上什么就是什么？鱼、我。

坐在酒吧前的俏女人过来问我是不是演电影的
女侠，在北京砖墙大院铁灰屋顶上飞奔？是啊，
梦的布景路过这河岸飞雪的小饭馆
是谁？曾经是谁？他、鱼。盘子里。

不管是谁，捕捉住，才是你的。写下
才活过。只是玻璃的海里，盛不下你，颂扬他
不如描述这把刀，先问问彼此的身份？炒作之后
依旧蒙着哪处的风沙？色味真地永不减褪？

那些辨不清的航线水情，转眼间使你和他
仇敌，兄弟，母女，悬在高处墙上眼神离散。
桌子上，最后的雪下个不停，串串黑脚丫
向东，向西，将通向那里的路一再掩埋。

3.

The implication is life was once honest—
anglers and writers, professions this city needs. Yet now
the catching of fish is no match for selling them, or the little show-off
served on the table. One look captures this season's fashion.

He once satisfied those on the water's edge, who followed Him
to heaven. Now I'm caught between drought and flood, between light
and its reflection, calculations, shouting myself hoarse, yet not knowing where to cast
the heart. Are we really whatever is caught, caught up? Fish, I.

The pretty woman at the bar comes to ask if I'm the GongFu heroine
in the movie, galloping over Beijing's gray roofs
and walled yards. Sure, this small restaurant beside the river under the drifting
snow passes for a dream stage. Who is it? Was it? Him, the fish in the dish.

No matter what it is, when it's caught, it's yours. Writing is living.
But the glass sea doesn't make you content. Praising Him proves no better
than describing this knife. First ask the identity of each. After flaying, the fish is still
covered with sand, and from where? The flavor doesn't fade?

These hidden sea routes make him your enemy, your brother, mother, daughters,
hanging on the wall, expressions blank. On the table, the last of the snow falls
constantly, where black footprints again bury
both ways: east and west, the way leads there.

translated by Susan M. Schultz

雨滴

迎着风走不难
只要克服阻力
顺着风行也不难
只需依从惯性
雨滴
悬置空间
往复不已
风从六面吹来

风从六面吹来
伞折了筋骨
变作雨的旗

A Raindrop

It's not difficult to go against the wind—
    just overcome the resistance.
It's not difficult to go *with* the wind either—
    merely obey inertia.

    A raindrop
    suspended in space
    winds back and forth
    the winds come from six directions.

Winds come from six directions
the fractured bones of an umbrella
become a flag—
stark banner of the rain.

translated by Leonard Schwartz

一 个 美 丽 的 早 晨

— 无名氏《雷霆：完美的精神》读后

一个美丽的早晨
昨夜　谁第一次如此排列辞句？
虚幻的景致　多日里惊雷滚动　风暴
推翻迟疑的枯叶和不确定的枝干。
解开扣紧的拘束，冰河上晨光斜射
小心探寻怎样欢庆眼前独一无二的现实？

梦一样陡现
大风中狂奔的女人
红衫　长发劲舞如蛇
不明身世掠过车窗玻璃
礼拜日　肃穆的反光——

　　　听我说！我来自动力原初，
　　　我来寻找寻找我的人。
　　　你看我　你看见你自己！
　　　不要反驳，你要恭敬！

清水浣洗　清水流。
早晨的世界没有诗　有奶
和女人和嗓音　柠檬香的肥皂
薄荷牙膏　一个半个五彩泡影
如远方信息　急切　迅速滑下视野。
女人的梦想变成男人的欲念后，
你止也止不住的心绪
在每一个早晨崭新地诞生。

Reading "Thunder: Perfect Mind"

A beautiful morning
late last night began: who first arranged the words
    this way?
Illusion landscape. Rolling thunder. Winter storm
blowing away timid leaves, hesitant stems,
unbuttoning each restraint.
    Morning light on the river.
Light searching out the way to celebrate
this unique.

As in a dream a woman appears
running in a gust of wind:
red shirt   long hair   dancing tongue
her unknown origin sweeps over Sunday,
its otherwise solemn reflections:

    LISTEN TO ME! I CAME FROM THE SOURCE OF POWER
    I SEEK OUT THOSE WHO SEEK ME.
    LOOK AT ME, YOU LOOK AT YOURSELF!
    DO NOT ARGUE! SHOW RESPECT!

Clear water washes. Clear water flows.
Morning world without poetry, milkless
And women's voices   lemon scented soap
Mint flavored toothpaste   two multi-colored bubbles
And news from afar eagerly awaited
vanishes from view
After the dream of woman turns into the desire of man
the emotion of an uncontainable mind
is reborn in each morning's freshness.

就在这里吗？
就是这唯一的早晨？

长早饭　浓咖啡　红茶
然后读报　写信
用粉红的纸　浅淡的水纹
然后听音乐
芬芳　一朵完美的玫瑰　伴二月南风
吹拂肌肤　忘形挑拨弹性的春情
眼神萦绕　清浅却欢欣流畅
自深远的背景里一再凸现。

> 我成功　我失败
> 智慧　却一无所知
> 沉默　而滔滔不绝
> 被污辱　被崇拜
> 我是土生土长的异乡人。

鸟鸣一颤而逝　抓不住
竟划下尖锐又肯定的图形　摇摆
软椅　孤寂的节拍
As if you know what I am thinking
鬼机灵
只为一种想象生活
投入一池纯粹的水或者风流的怀抱
游戏　完成一朵世纪末的玫瑰
枝桠尚未泛绿
你已经急急奏完了春曲:

> 我是圣女我是娼妓
> 我站在你全部恐惧的背后

Here?
This particular?

Long breakfast. Strong coffee. Black tea.
Read the newspaper. Write letters.
Pink paper with pale water marks.
Afterwards, listen to music.
Fragrance. A perfect rose. February's southwind
stirs the skin. Swiftly moving fingers
teasingly provoke the elastic love of spring.
The eye's expressivity lingers   clear and shallow
flows from the deep shadow raising up again:

> I AM SUCCESSFUL, I AM A FAILURE
> WISE YET UNKNOWING
> SILENT, CANNOT STOP TALKING.
> HUMILIATED, WORSHIPPED
> I WAS BORN AN ALIEN IN MY NATIVE LAND.

Birds cry and vanish, untrappable
yet discrete. Rocking.
Armchair. Desolation's rhythms.
"As if you know what I am thinking"—
How clever you are!
Live for this imagination. Desire only.
Dive to the absolute pool. Pure water's embrace.
A game. Perfect end-of-the-century rose.
Though the branches have not turned green
you have finished playing the spring sonata.

> I AM HOLY, I AM A WHORE.
> I STAND BEHIND ALL OF YOUR FEARS,

　　　　　我是你所有自信的源泉
　　　　　你要服从我！你要小心！

太阳透明地与我一起从屋外走过，猜不透
屋里孤独的集体秘密，乌鸦叫吉。
后院里茅草女巫手臂滴水
蓝风衣沉着脸迎面扑来
别吓唬我——没有女人　也没有孩子
街道铺张起坑坑洼洼的惶恐
吸引你步入湿润如夜的景深：
修道院改编博物馆　闪光的金属门面
晨钟和大风里狂奔的女人
肌肉搏动　细腰肢　紧乳房
千年精灵
你是她？

　　　　　我是生　我是死
　　　　　我最先　我最后
　　　　　我是每个声音的名字
　　　　　每个名字的声音　字和字间的空白
　　　　　只有我知道我的姓名！

半块吃剩的面包
驾潮流自西方向东挺进
以为有利可图。如果你能不嚼碎另外一半
避免冰凌表面耀眼的虚光　河底

I AM YOUR CONFIDENCE'S SOURCE.
YOU MUST OBEY— BE ON GUARD.

The sun and I walk cautiously
out of the room. Cannot figure out
the collective secret of the loneliness inside.
Crows cry. A good omen.
A straw witch stretches arms dripping water.
A navy windbreaker flaps at me.
You don't frighten me.
No women. No children either. Streets
spread terror, rough and bumpy,
attract your step into depths of field.
As wet as last night's warm rain.
Cloister changed into a museum, its shining metal facade.
The morning bell still faintly in the air
the woman running in a gust of wind.
Muscle contractions. Narrow waist. Tight breasts.
Spirit of a thousand years.
You are her?

I AM THE FIRST, I AM THE LAST.
I AM LIFE AND DEATH.
I AM THE NAME OF EVERY VOICE,
THE SOUND OF EVERY NAME
AND THE SPACE BETWEEN THE NAMES.
ONLY I KNOW MY OWN NAME.

Left over crust of bread
   riding the wave from west to east—
it seems there is a profit to be made.
If you won't chew the other half

静态的逻辑——水草　游鱼　咸腥的诗意
那么，这你与我的早晨
大风中狂奔的女人
也许会展示善意珍藏的精神：
呼吸起伏　温凉可触
哼着你为我作的短歌
以及精神以后无尽的变奏。

escape the glittering surface of the breaking ice.
Bottom of the river: static logic,
water grasses, fish and salty poetics
This morning of ours
as well as of the woman running in the gust of wind.
Inhales exhales heavily   tangible warmth
Hums the short song you wrote for me
with endless variations after the mind.

translated by Leonard Schwartz

女 人

—观 De Kooning《门系列》

1.

门敞开为某种流动，为裸露春的桃花。
呼吸里已经抹上一层新绿，诱惑嫩得出水。
对此强烈的季节在审视下愈加般配。

光深入敞开的门耍戏，却很真挚，
有皮肉齐笑的形象，龇玉兰瓣样的牙齿。
事实上，花朵大多纯色，并不花哨。

词迟迟不到。门敞开是因为笔触拥挤，
这不是一种线性或立体的进步，
颜料被它的外表一再否认，迈不出定义。

2.

门的外面是街和过时的每日新闻：
时装减价，比美大奖，新屋出售。
词与词面面相觑，无法从旧画报上复活。

在街边炫耀铺陈的水果摊上，
我苦苦寻找那只你切破的梨和窖藏的秩序。
行列被色块填满，绿苹果，橙桔，红樱桃。

视线的焦点从门移到街，以及街上行人，
获得的不仅是对事实的把握，
本来面目的认知穿起层次很多的衣服。

Doors

—after De Kooning

1.

The door opens to a certain flow, exposing the scent of spring peach,
Our breath already touched by new shades of green, temptation tender as water.
As we watch, the season's contrasting colors begin to match.

Light plays at the open door, albeit sincerely,
Bearing a toothy grin, magnolia petals between its lips.
These flowers are not gaudy, but pure.

Words come slowly. So many pen strokes oblige the door to open:
This is not progress, linear or three-dimensional.
A color denied surface cannot step outside its definition.

2.

Outside the door, the street, an old newspaper:
Discount fashions, beauty competitions, new houses for sale.
Word faces word, blankly; an old magazine refuses resurrection.

At the splendid fruit stands on the street
I patiently seek the pear you cut open and the orders you stashed in the cellar.
Rows of green, orange, cherry red.

Shift your focus from the door onto the street, its pedestrians;
Naked cognition puts on layers of clothing,
Gets hold of this reality.

3.

我忘记我是在画框里看水流。
意识躲躲闪闪，仿佛一团多边形的快感
羞怯地涌进另一味空间。门终于突破平面。

衣褶埋不住的燥热自腹股沟间勃起，
有什么被颠覆？有什么新生？
肥肿的胸腹和唇缘用力栽入门的深土。

没有人能逃出这四面林立的肉身。我无法呼吸。
必须为花与女人勾绘新的空维，以便盛开或结果，
并且从混杂，易变，色情，欺骗的语境中挣脱。

3.

I forgot I was watching water flow inside the picture frame.
Consciousness darts, as if pleasant and polygon-shaped,
Shyly swells into another dimension. The door breaks through this plane.

Heat, unstopped by fabric, rises from the crotch;
What was overturned, what reborn?
A swollen belly and lips push into the door's deep soil.

No one escapes this flesh from all sides. I can't breathe.
I must draw a new dimension for the woman so she can bloom or bear fruit,
Liberated from the semantics of the pornographic flower.

translated by Susan M. Schultz

妈妈事件

Mother Event

依 妹 通 讯

没有什么要讨论了。
还有吗？父亲？
草漫坡铺去，花也开过
阳光一格一格分配给
立正的楼群，也按时分给我一片
屏幕灰白——
还有什么要谈？
沉默，要说的失去
声音和真实感。你在家吗？
在家或走在很远的高山。狗
在长凳下嗅来嗅去
然后走开。麻雀几乎跳上你的肩
却没有。这时候我感到
真实的失去：
Bye, it is getting late
屏幕上传来前一个世界的黑甜。

eMail Correspondence

Not much to be discussed further
is there, Father?
Those long grasses spill over the hill, blooms blacken
in shadow as sunlight measured out square by square
the city at attention, in time to me, too
a patch of screen grayish white—
anything more to chat?
Whatever wants to be said loses
its voice and body.
Silence.

are you home?
Home, or hiking high mountains far away. A dog
snuffles around under the bench then
snuffles off. A sparrow tempted to jump to a shoulder
yet no. At that moment I feel the real loss:
good-bye, it is getting late
Darkness and a warm afterglow
close over the screen.

下　班

街上，车稠起来
匆匆走过的人，背着的背着
抱着的抱着，提着，挽着。
狗。邻居回来了，钥匙开门。
慢跑者穿了过长的短裤
晃出楼。

生活重新开始，人人一脸和气——
菜香，和送饭的小伙。
晚间新闻把白天发生的事
炒作一通端上桌。太阳下班
孩子们成群出动，叫、笑
树与树荫相亲相依
梦开始成真。

After Work

On the street, traffic thickens,
people jostle backpacked shoulders
bags clutched to chests, handles in hands, arms in arms.
Dogs. Neighbors return, keys click in doors.
Joggers sweat in their long shorts
waddle past the doorway.

Life sparks anew, peaceful faces smiling and polite
frying food smells, young deliveryman.
TV stir-fries today's events
sets them on the table. The sun punches out
children school up, cry, laugh
trees and their beloved shadows entwine as
dreams become true, after work.

translated by Bill Ransom

换 一 片 草

爬不出
狗或人尿过的草根
树，鸽子振臂升飞
在锅底，在摇篮旁边
看窗外草绿
孩子睡了，吃饱
家也干净，爬
爬不到光和风
飘扬的上面。接近
再接近一些，看清草芒
和蓬蓬的生命写成
与远处河水不动的呼应
一种。算了
就这样躺下，离去
有什么不好？美
已经很美：
居高，旁水，不多的花木
白石栏。
不遗忘现实——
家务，办公室，学话孩子
不安分的丈夫。
行饯，行饯，这最后一小时
丈量所有，修饰后院
为记住一切，在乎一切
还听见远驶的火车
出席牵牛花一个小时的盛筵
离去，离去
心情愉悦，光永存。

Grass Sprouting

can't crawl out
these grass roots peed on by dogs or human
tree, pigeons work their wings to take off
bottom of the pot, beside the crib
watch that grass greening outside the window
the child naps, curled and content
the house is clean.

can't crawl upward to
the flow of light and wind
Get close, closer, see clearly the grass blade
fluffy with life echo
that still river from afar
kind of. Let it be
lie down just like this, to leave
so why is it not good? Pretty
you are already beauty:
high perch, next to water, flowers and trees
and white stone fences.
Remember reality!
house chores, office, child learning to talk
husband restless.

Farewell dinner, farewell drink, one last hour
measures all, decorates this backyard
remember everything, care about everything
and hear that train rushing off
catch the one hour banquet of the morning glory
leave, leaving
delighted heart, light eternal.

体　检

还要在这里等多久？
写一首诗
减轻即将揭晓的未来。

一根蜂针刺入静脉
嗡地一响把心脏照亮——
（放射线与通常讲的情感无关）
屏幕上诱惑的绿蛇曲折。
监测。想吃禁果吗？
向上凸起阳刚——比如鸟劲舞的
翅膀。向下弯曲，接受流血的
事实，放松但并不表示
让步？忽而游走了，蜕下
一地苹果皮。

百叶窗外，几个少年
围着崭新的 Volkswagen
轮流到驾驶座坐一坐，摸摸
能摸到尾巴？藏到哪里啦？
苹果树不过刚刚开花。蜂拥。

加速，他伸出一根指头——
步子越密，要跑吗？登高
起步的时候总充满
早晨的信心，多么美
多么有力。看他们肩搭肩
一起抽纸烟，飘扬地吻吻彼此
唇瓣或毛茸茸的腮。
加速，两个指头
心跳，青信子伸缩
红灯
还有十秒钟。

Check-Up

How long do I have to wait here?
Write a poem
lighten these heavy prognostications.

The bee needle stabs a vein
"buzz" lights up the heart
(radiation isn't related to emotion, generally speaking.)
Seductive green snake curves across the monitor.
Want to eat the forbidden fruit?
Curve up? Yang and strength: bird's dancing
wings. Curve down? Accept the bleeding
to relax is no sign of giving up.
In a snap it swirls away, sheds skin
apple peels everywhere.

Outside the windowblind, youths
surround a brand new Volkswagen,
take turns in the driver's seat, touch here, there.
Have you touched the tail? Where is it hidden?
An apple tree buds out. Bees swarm.

Speed up. He extends one finger
steps quicken, have to run. Climb
At first, morning always filled us with
confidence, how beautiful
how strong! Watch them shoulder to shoulder
sharing a cigarette, so cool   kiss each other's
lip petals or fuzzy cheeks.
Speed up. Two fingers now
heart beats, blue fork tongue licks, contracts
the red light
still ten more seconds.

进入机器，雪白的金属臂
弯曲，把我抱紧，手放在头顶
暴露双腋，像小时候那样
毫无预想和戒心
（妈妈！）
心一下子
响起来
你的歌声，我的哭声，还有
粉红荧光指示剂
象征血（或者宝石）
在花枝上闪耀
青春，他的花园，即便
用金币堆出围墙，我依然
看见天真的光芒
期前收缩，四十年了
难道还能指望
更多？

我们要重新见面，少年，
信不信由你
你转过脸不看我，吐个烟圈
游弋，歧义，不眨又能怎么样？
就不回家
大星星亮了——

明天
我将等来生命的结果
少年将驾世界兜风
一切正常，一切正常
眯起没有眼睑的瞳孔
蛇
炫耀，秘不示人。

Enter the cold machine, white metal arms
curve, hold me tight, hands behind my head
expose both armpits, like when I was young
without warning or wariness
(Mom!)
heart suddenly
loud
Mom singing, my cries, and
the pink fluorescent dye
symbolizes blood (or rubies)
shines on the branches of flowering
youth, his garden, even if
surrounded by gold, I still
see the innocent glimmer
contracting ahead,
forty years of age
can I expect
more?

We will see each other again, youngster
believe or not
you turn and don't look at me, blow a smoke ring
swaying, divergent, not a blink, so what?
They won't go home
Star light, star bright.

Tomorrow the results from life.
These kids will take the world for a spin
everything is normal, everything's all right.
Narrowing those eyes without eyelids
snake, so flamboyant
scribbles out its secrets to no one.

translated by Bill Ransom

失 落 的 情 人

所有的失落集合
这棵树，为什么不？
在我窗前花开花落
已经为这么多鸟作窝、休脚。
一只、两只即兴的母狗走过，或
尿上一泡，并成为孩子们
橄榄球的家门。

会有一个地方，一弯天空
让他们集合，远远注视
假装不动声色的我，或
乔装之后走上前要个火，预先
知道豆萁早已焚烬。梦
会轻吻额头，演一出惊魂的
历险，让你再次游不出
泛光的湖。或命令你
数清所有树叶。落下
不觉中，你们全部落下
豆荚，在手中爆裂，亲亲
数不清的遗失变成我
醒来，面对此刻说不清的

白纸。

Lost Lovers

All life's losses gather
into this tree, and why not?
This nesting and rest stop for so many birds
blooms and sheds in front of my window.
Dogs in heat stroll by, pee
and children score their goals here.

There must be a place, a sliver of sky
for old loves to gather, staring from afar
pretending dispassion, maybe strolling over
under disguise to ask for a light, knowing
that the old beanstalk has long burnt to ash. Dreams
may still kiss the forehead, play out a dramatic
adventure (you again glide in the glittering lake
and can't swim out), or bid you to count out
a measure of brittle leaves. Falling,
unaware, you all fall down
beanpods pop in my hands, dearest—
this heap of losses becomes me
awake, facing this unsayable

blank page.

translated by Bill Ransom

玫 瑰 花 托

－给辛虹

修理轻舒的秀眉从事物阴影里
挑出甜酸对称的味道。茶杯来自日本
英格兰进口的茶和茶碟，乡间音乐
五十年代地歌颂正常生活，理直气壮。
这多日早晨的阳光也投在你的屏幕上？
隔一条河，几十条街，办公桌
肩搭肩不分彼此。把头发拢起，希望
再瘦一些，让脖子修长而且着重露出锁骨
给谁看？我们还能讨论什么——
除了异族男友，除了混血女儿？
这些贴肉的事物不留阴影，却牢牢
遮住我们的视线，像光针无辜地停在
时间的皱褶里，重复那个没有理由的音节：
eng eng eng eng

撒些胡椒粉，加糖，不易满足的胃口。
煎鸡蛋和才出烘箱的面包。先上什么呢？
侍者皱着眉。欲望不满足在街旁吠叫，又被
警车警笛卷走。马跑到哪里了？又有什么关系？
你说要等春天，暖和的日子
去学马术：皮靴硬帽，马裤夹克和小围巾
面对漫坡野花跑。我说自由不过是种想象——
这身套装正好紧绷绷
证明。而想象最好不去捉
因为谁也跑不脱自己两腿间的阴影。

Rose Hips

—for Camille

Elegant eyebrows pick up the shadow of things
well balanced flavor: sweet and sour. The tea cup, Japanese
the tea and saucer, English. Country music anthems
normal life in the fifties way, rightfully assured.
Does this winter morning sunlight warm your desk as well?
Separated by one river, a few blocks, desks
shoulder to shoulder almost a mirror. You do up your hair
to elongate your neck, expose collarbones, seem slimmer
for whom? What else can we discuss besides
boyfriends of different races, a daughter of mixed blood?
These things so close to flesh do not leave shadow, yet firmly
block our vision, as the needle of light trapped in
the soundtrack of time, repeating that nonsensical note
Eng Eng Eng Eng

Sprinkle on some pepper, and sugar, an appetite uneasy
tender eggs and bread fresh from the oven. What to serve first?
The waiter frowns. Desire barks on the street corner, then
flees ahead of the police siren. Where does the horse run? Does it matter?
You want to wait to learn to ride until the spring warm days:
boots and hard hat, breeches and flowery scarf through
wild flowers over the hill. I say freedom is only an
imagination as this tight-fit outfit perfectly
proves. Better not to catch the fantasy
for who can escape the shadow between our legs?
So we're pulled, dragged down desperate, table base
dark and heavy. Iron. Under the rose, a hip.

就这样，我们被拖住，被拼命往下拉，桌子
黑重的底座。铁。玫瑰底下的花托。

怎样才能摆脱天窗上巨大花环关于末日的恐吓：
卡在一个音节上也不能让我们永远纤瘦，永远
没有阴影地笑。手边的茶杯茶碟定义
现实的秩序和必须的无足轻重——
困境：太长的生命，太少的感情
困境：太短的生命，太多的感情

是的，我们矛盾，解不开，逃不掉
像阳光从我的桌面移到你的桌面
明亮却在郁金香的厚叶子上映出花瓣的
碎影。花瓶随意站着，与糖罐相隔不可能
缩短的距离。我们对眼前的事物
无从下手，不是到得太早就是来得太晚
虽然我们只想活在现在，只想生活在
还没有影子的一瞬间。

还是写吧，用中文或者英文，用与生命
合辙的音韵。失去光彩的事物并不失落倒影。
花开过，才有这有滋有味的花托在
杯底泛起粉红的回忆。不是吗？冒泡的情绪
正冒起蒸汽。我们可以用带口音的发言讲清楚
即便只是我们的问题。重复，如果必须
重复。忘记眼前这些无从下手的点缀
如果必须。也许只有生活在回忆里
句子才能稳住脚跟
　　　　在忧郁的土中
　　　　　　　在书桌下面。

How to exorcise the doomsday horror
of that giant garland on the window:
stuck on a single syllable doesn't allow us to be slender forever, forever
smiling without shadow. The tea cup and saucer near your hand define
the reality of order and the necessity of the weightlessness

Difficult situation: live too long, feel too little.
Difficult situation: live too short, feel too much.

Yes, we are conflicted, unresolved, unable to escape
like sunlight moves from my desk to yours
bright yet on the thick leaves of the tulip cast the broken shadows of
petals. Flower vase stands freely, separated from the sugar jar
by an uncrossable distance. We can't handle things
in front of our eyes, arriving too early or coming too late
though we only want to live in the present, only at this
moment while there are yet shadows.

Let's just write, in Chinese or English, use vocabulary
in rhyme with life. Those things that lost their shine
do not lose their shadows.
Only after the bloom, come the tasty hips
suffusing pink memories from the bottom of the cup.
Isn't it from the bubbly emotion
steam rises? We can, with our accent, speak clearly
if only of our problems. Repeat, if we must
repeat. Forget the helpless frivolousness at hand.
Maybe only by living through memory
the sentence can steady its soles
    in the melancholy soil
        under our desks.

translated by Bill Ransom

最 重 的 东 西

－给马兰

把最重的东西挖出来
放进嘴里，喝下去
是欲望，从左心房流向右心房：
一只手听不懂另一只手的
心痛。感觉呢？滑到
你的独木舟底，刻出
这永不忘怀的水。

雨下落不明。最重的
不是你写下的故事，也不是
你在越洋电话里的声音。苦闷
其实很轻，能说出的都轻。轻得像虹
在安地高山上喘不过气时，从指缝间
蓝空气里滴下来——
一定是你雨点般扑向我面前的阳光。

让他们爬上爬下像这些顽石
被你磨得柔情万种：
不过，要想突出自己的位置
就再也无法挤入你的腹地。不由地向上
迭起这祭神的屋宇。而你和他们肢体镶嵌！
肢体镶嵌像磨合的石壁，像理念交错的
句法不透风地将故事女主人公重重包围。

旗举在头上最高，却不一定最重。
他说结论是假的。我说故事

The Heaviest Thing

—for Malan

Dig out the heaviest thing
stuff it into your mouth, drink down
desire, drifting from left atrium to the right atrium:
one hand can't comprehend the other hand's
stony, sorrowful heart. Emotion? Slide
under the bottom of your log boat, carve out
this stark unforgetting water.

Rain sweeps into the dark. Heavy
is neither the stories you write nor
your voice over the sea. Depression
in fact is very light, whatever can be said
is light. As light as that rainbow
on an Andes mountain, breathless, between your fingers
trickling down from the blue air—
you throw yourself into the sun right in front of me.

Let them climb up and down these boulders
you polished so smooth and gentle:
still, if they want elevation they surrender
the squeeze near your navel, pile up
pile upward these structures of worship. You and they
body-limb enlaced!
Bodies and limbs inlaid like stones of a wall, concepts-locked
sentences wind-tight cocoon the heroine of your stories.

The highest banner above the heads is
not necessarily the heaviest.

必定真实。"好累哟",你咯咯地笑。
你只把它挂在嘴边。笑得响了
也许就得救了。可他们非要在你脸上
蒙住麻醉面罩,那时候你抓起笔
你数:一、二、三……
哗——
吹放一池荷花:荷花少女
　　　　　　捏着她的红纸
　　　　　　　　　　清水轻浮。

He says your conclusion is fake. I say the stories
must be true then. "So boring," you laugh.
You hang your ha!ha!ha! around the corner of your mouth.
Laugh louder and be saved!
But they insist on the mask, the anesthesia
you grab a pen
you count: one, two, three ...
"Hey!"—
bloom open a pond of lotus: Lotus Girl
        two fingers pinch her red paper
            limpid water, a flirtatious light.

translated by Bill Ransom

妈 妈 事 件

一给玉然

当妈妈了

坐在上面的感觉是旋晕——
那么小，那么软软
肉
咬在嘴里
一肚子　　　水

～

一开始
他们把一次用无菌塑料管
从纸套里
一下子
撕出来——
（像在案板上剥鸡皮）
没有多余动作
漂
屋顶，房梁，牛羊
从水床陷下去
自然
而不流于
生灵、感情
他们不断地换纸衬
改写天蓝
说出的完美：

Mother Event

—for YuRan

Mother now

      dizzying sensation of sitting on high—

          so small, so soft

flesh

      a bite in the mouth

          a belly of   water

∽

to begin

they peel out the sterile plastic pipette

      from its paper wrapper

      in a single motion—

(like stripping chicken from its skin)

          no wasted movement

float

      roof, pillar, sheep and cows

          sink from the waterbed

natural

      not yet flooded with

          spirit or mood

they repeatedly change the paper pads

      rewrite the sky-blue

          the language of perfection:

separate out this distinct contour   you

      slippery in a sheet of cream

      freshly minted nailtips:

          one, two, three, four, five

分出分明的你
　　　　光溜溜擦着一身白脂
　　　　崭新的尖指甲：
　　　　　　　一二三四五

光　　　　　　全景
所有的蓝：
沙发、长袍、手套、床垫、毯子、小毛帽
衬托
　　　　一点点肉
　　　　　　（蓝）
　　　　　　　　　　眼睛（蓝）

～

谁让
他们把你推去
　　　　　抽血！
　　　　　　吸脊髓！
　　　　　　　装进玻璃隔离箱！
　　　　　　　胸脯上贴电极！
　　　　　　　脚丫几块血痂！
抱起来
　　　　贴肉
（连着那些管子、电线、显示器）
吸　　胸脯的两眼　　紧得痛
拒绝赝品
　　　　大哭
　　　　大抖
　　　　（还会咳嗽！）——
　　　　　　　　　把肉给我！

～

light   panorama
all blue:
sofa, gowns, gloves, mattress pad, blankets, tiny terry-cloth hat
sets off
       a bit of flesh
           (blue)
               eyes (blue)

~

who let them
take you away—
     Draw blood
        Tap spine
          Stick electrodes to chest
            Seal into the glass incubator
               Bloody stains on tiny feet!

Hold it up
against the skin
(a clutter of tubes, wires, monitors)
suck eyes of the breasts   throbbing tight
refuse the fake
     loud cry
     violent shake
     (it can cough, too!)—
         return me my flesh!

~

他说
"是我先看见头发， 黑　头发"
还有　"血"
血？
还有　"喊""哭"
哭？　喊？

～

咱们回家吧
嗯
离开这个太多手的地方
　　　　　　　　　　　太亮太闹
下雨也好，天热也好
　　　咱们有窗　　百叶窗
　　　摇篮　毛毯　关灯

～

会哭　却没有泪
（像上弦的炸弹，却不定时）
饿了　　　　哭
尿　　　　　　　　　哭
累　哭
困　　　　　　　　　　哭
高兴
（在缺乏表达的时候　　不笑）
穿衣服　　　　　　哭
换尿片　　　哭　　　　哭　哭
趴下　哭

he says—
"I saw the hair first, black   hair"
                              "blood"
blood?
                    "screams" and "cries"
Cries? Screams?

⌣

let's go home
OK
leave this place full of hands
                                        too bright too noisy
whether rain or heat
          we have a window, with shades
              bassinette   blankets   turn off the light

⌣

it can cry   without tears
(like a bomb already set, but with an erratic timer)
hungry   cry
wet   cry
tired   cry
sleepy   cry
delighted
(when lacking means of expression   it doesn't smile)
dressing   cry
full diaper   cry   cry   cry
belly down   cry
held up against the chest
up and down

抱起来　　　贴胸
上上下下

　　　　　　　　　哭

　　哭

～

不哭的时候
也（会）　　看我
　　　谁的眉毛　　眼角？
把门开开
　　　让"我"进来
眼睛的眼睛
没有距离地明澈　　把我藏起
是我！　　　（是我的？！）

放下－放不下的镜子
小手　小脚　小兔子
捏紧拳头
臭臭地
分不开
　　　　　　　　　下雨了
哗啦哗啦　　　　水
一个小蜘蛛
　　　滚下坡

～

                              cry
              cry
    ～

when not crying
it (can) look at me
              those eyelids
Open the door
              let "me" in
eye of eyes
clarity of no distance   hide me
is me!   (is this mine!)

put this mirror down—can't
little hands   little feet   a little bonnie
tight fists
stinky
won't open up

                    it rains
hualahuala   water
a little spider
              slides down the hill

    ～

these faces
dark, wrinkled, fat and thick, powder soiled
once held to breasts, kissed and kissed again?
This perfection of mother's bosom
would stand in lines
              to join these faces
                              on the bus?

这些脸
暗、皱、肥厚、不干净的脂粉
原来都曾搂在怀里　　亲了又亲？
妈妈怀里的完美
也会排队
　　　　排起队加入这些脸
　　　　　　　　坐车？

不许他们看
看你　永远粉红轻浅的呼吸
水一样的腮
野百合从胸脯直铺向
　　　　胖腿
　　　　　　小小的
　　　　　　　　　岔开。

因为你是不一样的。

不一样的干净
不一样的感觉。

〜

这些你
这些我
一、二、三、四、五
　　　　　　六、七
马兰开花二十一
　　　　　　还有
　　　　　　　　这些一

don't let them watch
watch you   breaths shallow, light pink, eternal
cheeks of water
wild lilies spread from chest to
       chubby legs'
          little
               fork.

Because you are not the same.

Not the same clean
not the same perception.

∽

these you
these I
one, two, three, four, five
        six, seven
all pretty orchids
        go to heaven

∽

The expression of no "I"
how can that be called an expression
       is the loveliest expression
          is the only possible expression

∽

～

没有　我（！）的表情
怎么能叫表情
　　　　　　是最可爱的表情
　　　　　　　是唯一可能的表情

～

我也曾如此享用
　　　这重复不尽的
捧、拍、抱、举、摇、搂、背、扛、抬
擦、洗、抹、刷、梳、捋、晃、亲、吻
笑容、奶水、歌唱——
　　　永远地好心情　　　没脾气
　　　累得困得倦得厌得不能耐时再要永远继续？

不记得吃你的奶
　　　"吃到一岁半呐"
不记得吃屎
　　　"吃得满脸都是"
记得尿床
　　　"不记得你长牙的历史"
胖肚子、小眼睛、粗嗓子、大个子
（想起来了没有？）
所以后来长成美人坯子——
　　　鸭蛋脸、柳腰、长腿、细踝

这些不被记住的事迹
才让我们

in the past did I, too, enjoy
        this endless
hold, pat, embrace, carry, rock, hug, piggyback
clean, wash, rub, brush, comb, stroke, kiss, smooch
smile, breastfeed, sing—
        always a good mood   no temper
        always keep up even when tired, sleepy, exhausted, bored and can't
                stand one second more?

Don't recall drinking your milk
        "'till you're a year and a half"
don't remember eating my duty
        "all over your face"
remember the accidents at night
        "don't remember your teething history"
fat belly, small eyes, thick voice, big girl
(do you remember now?)
so later on it grew into beauty itself—
        oval face, willowy waist, long legs, delicate ankles

these victories forgotten
        allow us
                to grow up without turning back
                        temperamental and with no patience?

Achievements left you
        are not you
                only suspicions—
you did hold me tight
        (even if I don't remember and cried my best)
you held me in good spirits
didn't toss me into the river
                                mom

不回头地长大
　　　　耍脾气并且缺乏耐心？
事迹离开你
　　不是你
　　　　仅仅疑问——
你的的确确紧紧地抱过我
　　（即便我不记得而且大哭）
　　好心情地抱过我
　　没有把我丢下河
　　　　　　妈妈

∽

这结晶的
眼泪
和
所有的
爱情！

与你个性的故事无关——
　　　　生命的表达还原如此单纯——
　　　　值得掂量的仅仅是
　　　　　　体重
　　　　　　　你为什么只喜欢天蓝色
　　　　　　今天吃了几盎司　　　果泥？

∽

一二三四五
上山找老虎　（不能打了，PC）
老虎不在家

~

these crystallized
tears
and
all
that love!

Has nothing to do with your personal story
　　　the manifestation of life reduces to purity—
　　　all there is worth measuring is
　　　　　　body weight
　　　　　　why you only like blue
　　　　　　how many oz. of mashed fruit you ate today?

~

one two three four five
climb the slope where the tigers live　　(of course not to hunt, PC)
don't see tiger slinking around
so plant this watermelon　　　　　　(Hey, Hey)
melon grows no melon seeds
becomes a turtle in the reeds　　(Hey, Hey)!

Hmmmm, BaoBao
sleep
sleep
BaoBao

~

种下棵大西瓜　　　　（嘿嘿）
西瓜没结籽儿
变了个大王八　　　　（嘿嘿）！

嗯，宝宝
睡
睡
宝宝

缺乏某种节奏
是否便是　　　节奏？

咸甜苦辣
成了多余的添加：
　　　　　　双眼皮黏着
　　　　　　　　米粉和豌豆泥
引得妈妈舔：
　　　　吱吱尖叫　　　嘿嘿
别去抓眼睛

～

这撕肝
　　裂胆的
爱
　　　和
　　不能
　　　　分离
　　　的

lack of any rhythm
is it   the rhythm?

Salty sweet bitter spice
become superfluous:
        double-fold eyelids sticky with
                rice flakes and mashed peas
draw mom's tongue:
           squeaks   Hey, Hey
don't scratch your eyes

∼

this love
        tears
and
        a bundle
            that can't
        be
separated!

Hands that hold you tight
        throw you down the river
            now
                or later
you assume
she will recognize you?
on the road?
        Girls
           born
                die
                    born again …

一团！

抱紧你的手
　　　　把你丢下河
　　　　　　或早

　　　　　　　　或晚
你以为
她能认出你？
在路上？
　女孩子
　　　　生生

　　　　　　死死

　　　　　　生生……
为什么不可以

　　　　　　永远
　　　　　女儿？
你
凭什么剥夺我
　　　　　每三小时
　　　　　你占一小时？

哭
　　　你还哭
　　　　　我为什么不能？

〜

（这弯在我肩头曲线的重量

　　　　　　　　　　　　柔和）
你额头

why not
　　　eternally
　　　　　the daughter?
You
what right do you have to rob me
　　　　　one hour
　　　　　of every three?
Cry
　　　you still cry
　　　　　why can't I?

~

(the weight of this curve on my shoulder

　　　　　　　　　　　　　　　soft)

your forehead
shines
compare it to   what?

A leopard cub
prickly claws
two bloody scratches ...

~

days not needing sugar
　　　　　　are not bitter
days of milk
　　　white and pink
　　　　　a chin dripping drool
no one can compare to you
　　　embrace you　　　　embrace self

光亮
能　　　　　　比　　　　　什么？
小豹子
细小的爪子
两道血印……

～

不加糖的日子
　　　　　　　　不苦
奶的日子
　　　　白与粉红
　　　　　　　　下巴粘了涎水
没有谁能和你比
　　　　拥抱你　　　　　　　拥抱自己
新生：滚圆的肚皮，盘曲的腿，温柔的思路，不可能的情

挖个大坑
　　　　埋掉你　　　　　我的身体
　　　　以及
记忆：孩子和母亲的故事
　　　　这贴肉的　　　　　位置与人称

惊人的水注入
　　　　　　都淹掉
　　　　　　　　　　淹掉

因为这不可能

newborn: pouched belly, crossed legs, tender thoughts, impossible feeling

Dig a big hole
      bury you   my body
      and
this memory: the story of mother and child
      flesh-and-blood their positions and personal pronouns

surprising water rises
        all drown
                      drown

because it is not possible

translated by Bill Ransom

软席候车室叙事

二叔二婶陷在皮沙发里
宽大地微笑。不愧是老铁道
在涌来涌去的混乱中，一针把大车站的
牛皮戳破，舒服地坐下去
等我们定下神再继续两年前的谈话："那里已经没草了
　　　，沙化，他们说"。
才写了几首诗，生了个孩子，就没草了？

暴雨打在蒙古包上，暴雨的羊
穿碧绿长裙金马甲的红脸小姑娘？

二叔没变，又胖了，"只吃菜
不吃饭也胖"，全球减肥的难题。
"什么都可以吃，什么都不要多吃"
我听见自己说。希望真理就这么简单——
而我现在就想吃禁忌的冰激凌
难以分离的手感在屁股上变成累赘
我身体罪恶又最不明朗的一部分。

怎么办？恐怖分子，感情陷井，经济危机
晚生的孩子，抑郁症，失眠，失眠……

In the Soft Sleeper Waiting Lounge

Second Uncle Second Aunt sink
into leather sofa which generously sighs.
First Class Waiting Lounge. Hooray! Working
on the railroad, all the live long day long. Easy
enough to puncture hauptbanhof. Thick dermis.
Comfortably arrayed around this secret
the chaos of outside tides in tides out.
—pause—waits for us to calm all the way down. Now
continue conversation
started two years ago: "There is no grassland any more,
      desertization they say."
              Wrote a few poems,
              had a child,
                      now there's no grass left?

Rain beats down on yurt, a sheep of rain—
where's ruby-faced girl in long apple
green skirt, gold-trimmed vest?

Second Uncle hasn't changed, only fatter, "Eat only vegetable dishes,
no more rice, still get fat!" The easier said than done problem of global diet,
solved: "Eat everything, overeat nothing," I hear myself saying—
wish a simple truth—now time for forbidden maple ice-cream!
Hand inseparable from butt grows into a burden,
a part of my body shameful, ambivalent.

What to do? Terrorists, emotional trap, recession,
late born child, depression, insomnia, insomnia …

二叔消瘦的时候反右，犯错误，离婚
支边放羊，（像我现在一样），本来铁定的
结果，却像那只童话里的聚宝盆：
"拉出一个老头，又一个老头……"

抓住一根贪婪的尾巴，举起道德的鞭
二叔讲故事的时候却总是笑呵呵的
讲一次笑一次——

平时背得重，出门越提越少，二叔。
我现在也有这种趋向。

When Second Uncle was thin, anti-rightist movement, committed mistakes, divorced,
transported to border region to herd sheep, the iron-
clad conclusion – ah! it's the fable's ever-full treasure chest!
She pushes her annoying old man in, accidentally
during their fight over what is the worthiest thing to put in
and what does she pull out? Why, the old man after the old man!
Catch the tail of greed, the whip of ethics.
Second Uncle always laughs
when he tells the Husband Parade story,
laughs over and over when he tells—

Every day he shoulders the heavy heavy,
so when he travels he
carries less and less, Second Uncle;
I myself have the same tendency now.

translated by Bob Holman

四哥

肯定是那顶鸭舌帽
在暗中使劲，他有把握地走近：
"你们也回？南坡李家？"
怎么会看不出来，一家人
笑得都像。其它深层的表情和着
慢车摇曳的拍子，模糊出
满座席温柔的背景，阳光

从早晨到正午，聊家里的事——
黄土坡，窑洞，道边的树一闪一闪

像没有注册的偏方，贴得满街晃眼
谜底却藏在你手里，自己研制
又一说是祖传，就好比根深叶茂的
道理和一针就好的性病，支持
我们深信的模糊逻辑。打烧饼的
医师助理和正在进行时的葬礼
信与不信，日子一样过得端正正。

只有一个表面，四哥的侧脸肖像
右边过道该是我拍照，也面目晴朗？

On the Train: Fourth Brother

The cap's beak must have exerted a
quiet pressure—Fourth Brother confidently approaches:
"You on your way home too? You're Li family, NanPo, south slope, yes?"
Of course he can tell, family
even smile the same way. Under smile,
other expressions of molecular genetics syncopate
shrugs to the slow train's
swaying rhythm. Sound blurs visuals,
the background of the soft sleeper softens. Sun.

Morning till noon, chatter gossip—
yellow soil, caves' people build houses into hills,
a geologic fact, trees track along the flicker …

Local folk medicine advertised all over town, dazzling.
The real cure is in your hands, did the research yourself!
Or—legend has it that your ancestors passed the secret down to you.
Folks, the prowess of this remedy is so strong, these here leaves so fecund
that one punctuation of acupuncture and your STD's will be banished forever!
Take a deep breath of the profoundly ambiguous logic we believe in.

Like flipping a wheat cake, the doctor's assistant
and the funeral coexist in present tense—believe it!
or don't, life g-g-g-going on, eminently

stable.

There's only one surface
and that's Fourth Brother's silhouette.

I was the one who took the picture, on the other
side of the passageway. The same sunny expression
in my face, in my eyes?

translated by Bob Holman

决定

放下去的
天，碧蓝如我们相识的
下午，等待
意外让我们走到一起
再各自走开。可以给出
一切，却决定什么都
不给。微笑着走开
去拥抱街上婚车喇叭
决定地一路欢乐。
不过是风
不能决定自己
树叶在室外小幅度摆动
不小心擦过这扇蒙尘的窗
划破多年哀怨。
感谢失控
是一个决定：
右转弯。这样
剪接技术就能救我们——
记录过去和将来
这就是全部。翻过

Resolution

Put it down
to the sky
turquoise and transparent
like the afternoon
we met, wait
this time let us
walk towards each other
and keep walking.
Could give everything,
but nothing. Walk
on by, smile, OK, whirl
to the horns
of the wedding procession
damn cheerful all the way.
It is only the wind
that can't control itself. Leaves
make tiny lapping waves outside,
unintentionally brush dust
from the window, and then
Cut to sepia: accumulated sadness.
Resentment even. Crap
indignation. OK, be grateful
for this loss of control
go on go ahead make a right
turn. This way
the montage technique will save us—
graft the past on the future,
that's all. Turn over
the present, blaze dance
of unknowing branches

现在，以及
枝条在阳光里不知情的
舞蹈。决定——
吃东西
写这些句子。四两轻。

in the sun. Resolved:
eat something. Resolved:
write these sentences.
Light as feather.
Four ounces.

translated by Bob Holman

AUTHOR

Zhang Er was born in Beijing, China and moved to New York City in 1986. Her writings of poetry, non-fiction, and essays have appeared in publications in Taiwan, China, the American emigre community and in a number of American journals. She is the author of multiple books in Chinese and in English translation. She has read from her work at international festivals, conferences, reading series and universities in China, France, Portugal, Russia, Peru, Singapore, Hong Kong as well as in the U.S. She currently teaches at The Evergreen State College in Washington.

TRANSLATORS

Bob Holman's eighth book, *A Couple of Ways of Doing Something*, a collaboration with Chuck Close, was published in 2003. He was a founder of Mouth Almighty/Mercury Records, the first major label devoted to poetry. He is Chief Curator of the People's Poetry Gathering, Poetry Guide at About.com, and Proprietor of the Bowery Poetry Club (bowerypoetry.com). He was recently appointed Visiting Professor of Writing at Columbia University, and received the 2003 Barnes & Noble "Writers for Writers" Award.

Arpine Konyalian Grenier, author of *St. Gregory's Daughter and Whores of Samarkand*, is a graduate of the American University of Beirut and the MFA Program at Bard College, New York. Her work has appeared in *Columbia Poetry Review, The Iowa Review, Phoebe and Kiosk*.

Timothy Liu's first book of poems, *Vox Angelica* (Alice James Books, 1992), received the Norma Farber First Book Award from the Poetry Society of America. His subsequent books of poems are *Burnt Offerings* (Copper Canyon Press, 1995) *Say Goodnight,* (Copper Canyon Press, 1998), and *Hard Evidence* (Talisman House, 2001). Tenured at William Paterson University, Liu lives in Manhattan.

Bill Ransom has published six novels and six collections of poems, including *Finding True North* from Copper Canyon Press, which was nominated for both the Pulitzer Prize and the National Book Award. His novel *Jaguar* was recently re-released by Wildside Press. He is a member of the faculty at The Evergreen State College.

Susan M. Schultz is the author of multiple poetry and essay collections, most recently *And Then Something Happened* (Salt, 2004) and *A Poetics of Impasse in Modern and Contemporary American Poetry* (Alabama, 2005). She edited *The Tribe of John: Ashbery and Contemporary Poetry* (Alabama, 1995). She founded Tinfish Press, which publishes a journal and chapbooks featuring experimental work from the Pacific. Schultz is Professor of English at the University of Hawai`i-Manoa.

Leonard Schwartz is the author of several collections of poetry, most recently *Ear and Ethos* and *The Tower of Diverse Shores* (Talisman House). He is also the author of a collection of essays *A Flicker At The Edge Of Things: Essays on Poetics 1987-1997* (Spuyten Duyvil) and co-editor of two anthologies of contemporary American poetry: *Primary Trouble: An Anthology of Contemporary American Poetry* and *An Anthology of New (American) Poets* (both from Talisman House). He teaches at The Evergreen State College in Washington.